INFORMATION AND NETWORK SECURITY

NETWORK SECURITY

AF551891

DR. MANMOHAN SINGH | DR. MONIKA VYAS | DR. RICHA CHAUDHARY | DR. JITENDRA MALVIYA

Copyright © Dr. Manmohan Singh, Dr. Monika Vyas, Dr. Richa Chaudhary, Dr. Jitendra Malviya
All Rights Reserved.

This book has been published with all efforts taken to make the material error-free after the consent of the author. However, the author and the publisher do not assume and hereby disclaim any liability to any party for any loss, damage, or disruption caused by errors or omissions, whether such errors or omissions result from negligence, accident, or any other cause.

While every effort has been made to avoid any mistake or omission, this publication is being sold on the condition and understanding that neither the author nor the publishers or printers would be liable in any manner to any person by reason of any mistake or omission in this publication or for any action taken or omitted to be taken or advice rendered or accepted on the basis of this work. For any defect in printing or binding the publishers will be liable only to replace the defective copy by another copy of this work then available.

This book is dedicated to help educators teach classes in the Security environment. It introduces Information and Network Security and their application in e-learning.

Contents

Preface

Network Security enables simplified functionality of infrastructure and platforms used in IT and IT-enabled industries, so that the end-users can avail what they want and pay only for the service they use.

Information and Network Security can be characterized as Internet-based computing in which many remote servers are networked to enable shared data-processing ventures, centralized knowledge storage, and access to services or resources online.

CHAPTER ONE

Symmetri Cipher Model

Basics of Information and Network Security

- In daily life we use information for various purposes and use network for communication and exchange information between different parties.
- In many cases these information are sensitive so we need to take care that only authorized party can get that information.
- For maintaining such privacy we require some mechanism or physical device which ensures that it is safe. Such mechanism or physical devices are known as **security system.**
- **Computer Security:** The protection afforded to an automated information system in order to attain the applicable objectives of preserving the **integrity**, **availability**, and **confidentiality** of information system resources.
- This definition of computer security introduces three key objectives that are at the heart of computer security:

1. **Confidentiality:** It covers two concepts

Data Confidentiality: Assures that private or confidential information is not made available or disclosed to unauthorized individuals.

Privacy: Assures that individuals control or influence what information related to them may be collected and stored and by whom and to whom that information may be disclosed.

1. **Integrity:** It covers two concepts

Data Integrity: Assures that information and programs are changed authorize manner.

only in a specified and

System Integrity: Assures that a system performs its intended function in an unimpaired manner, free from deliberate or inadvertent unauthorized manipulation of the system.

3. **Availability:** Assures that systems work promptly and service is not denied to authorize user.

- **Unconditionally secure algorithm:** An algorithm or an encryption scheme is unconditionally secure if the attacker cannot obtain the corresponding plaintext from ciphertext no matter how much ciphertext is available.
- **Computationally secure algorithm:** An encryption scheme is said to be computationally secure if either of the following criteria is met:

◦ The cost of breaking the cipher exceeds the value of the encrypted information.

- The time required to break the cipher exceeds the useful lifetime of the information.

- **Threat:** A potential for violation of security, which exists when there is a

circumstance, capability,
action, or event that could breach security and cause harm. That is, a threat is a possible danger that might exploit vulnerability.

Security Attacks

- **Security Attacks:** An attack is an action that comprises the information or network security.
- There are two types of attacks:

1. Passive Attack
2. Active Attack

Passive Attack

- **Passive Attack:** The attacker

only monitors the traffic attacking the confidentiality of the data. It
contains release of message contents and traffic analysis (in case of encrypted data).

1. Release of message contents:

- The release of message contents is easily understood.

- A telephone conversation, an electronic mail message, and a transferred file may contain sensitive or confidential information.

-

  We would like to prevent an opponent from learning the contents of these transmissions.

2. Traffic analysis:

   - A second type of passive attack, traffic analysis.
   - Suppose that we had a way of masking the contents of messages or other information.
   - Even if they captured the message, could not extract the information from the message.

- The common technique for masking contents is encryption.
- If we had encryption protection in place, an opponent might still be able to observe the pattern of these messages.
- The opponent could determine the location and identity of communicating hosts and could observe the frequency and length of messages being exchanged.
- This information might be useful in guessing the nature of the communication that was taking place.
- Passive attacks are very difficult to detect because they do not involve any alteration of the data.
-

Typically, the message traffic is send and received in an apparently normal fashion and the sender nor receiver is aware that a third party has read the messages or observed the traffic pattern.

Active attack

- **Active attack:** Attacker tries to alter transmitted data. It includes masquerade, modification, replay and denial of service.

1. **Masquerade:** A masquerade takes place when one entity pretends to be a different entity (Figure a). A masquerade attack usually includes one of the other forms of active attack.

2. **Replay:** Replay involves the passive capture of a data unit and its subsequent retransmission to produce an unauthorized effect.

3. Modification of messages:

    - Modification of messages simply means that some portion of a legitimate message is altered, or that messages are delayed or reordered, to produce an unauthorized effect (Figure c).
    - For example, a message meaning "Allow John Smith to read confidential file accounts" is modified to mean "Allow Fred Brown to read confidential file accounts."

4. Denial of service:

    - The denial of service prevents or inhibits the normal use or management of communications facilities.

    - This attack may have

a specific target; for example, an entity may suppress all messages directed to a particular destination (e.g., the security audit service).

◦

Another form of service denial is the disruption of an entire network, either by disabling the network or by overloading it with messages so as to degrade performance.

Security services

- A security service is a processing or communicating service that can prevent or detect the above- mentioned attacks. Various security services are:

- **Authentication:** the recipient should be able to identify the sender, and verify that the sender, who claims to be the sender, actually did send the message.
- **Data Confidentiality:** An attacker should not be able to read the transmitted data or extract data in case of encrypted data. In short, confidentiality is the protection of transmitted data from passive attacks.
- **Data Integrity:** Make sure that the message received was exactly the message the sender sent.

- **Nonrepudiation:** The sender should not be able to deny sending the should not be able to deny receiving the message.

message. The receiver

Symmetric Cipher Model

- A symmetric cipher model are broadly contains five parts.
- **Plaintext:** This is the original intelligible message.

- Encryption algorithm: The

encryption algorithm performs various substitutions and
transformations on the plaintext. It takes in plaintext and key and gives the ciphertext.

- **Secret key:** The key is a value independent of the plaintext and of the algorithm. Different keys will yield different outputs.
- **Ciphertext:** This is the scrambled message produced as output. It depends on the plaintext and the secret key.

- Decryption algorithm: Runs

on the ciphertext and the key to produce
the plaintext. This is
essentially the encryption algorithm run in reverse.

- Two basic requirements of encryption are:

1. Encryption algorithm should be strong. An attacker knowing the algorithm and having any number of ciphertext should not be able to decrypt the ciphertext or guess the key.
2. The key shared by the sender and the receiver should be secret.

- Let the plaintext be $X = [X1, X2,..., X_M]$, key be $K = [K1, K2,..., K_J]$ and the ciphertext produced be $Y = [Y1,$

  $Y2,..., Y_N]$. Then, we can write

$$Y = E(K, X)$$

- Here E represents the encryption algorithm and is a function of plaintext X and key K.
- The receiver at the other ends decrypts the ciphertext using the key.

$$X = D(K, Y)$$

- Here D represents the decryption algorithm and it inverts the transformations of encryption algorithm.
- An opponent not having access to X or K may attempt to recover K or X or both.
- It is assumed that the opponent knows the encryption (E) and decryption (D) algorithms.

- If the opponent is interested

  in only this particular message, then the focus of the effort is to

  recover by generating a plaintext estimate ^X.

- If the opponent is interested in being able to read future messages as well then he will attempt to recover the key by making an estimate ^K.

Cryptography

- **Cryptography:** The area of

study containing the principles and methods of transforming an

intelligible message into one that is unintelligible, and then retransforming that message back to its original form.

- Cryptographic systems are characterized along three independent dimensions.

1. **The types of operations used for transforming plaintext to ciphertext.** All encryption algorithms are

   based on two general principles substitution, and transposition. Basic requirement is that no

   information be lost. Most systems referred to as product system, involves multiple stages of

   substitutions and transpositions.

2. **The number of keys used.** If both sender and receiver use the same key, the system is referred to as **symmetric, single-key, secret-key, or conventional encryption.** If the sender and receiver use different keys the system is referred to as **asymmetric, two-key, or public-key encryption.**
3. **The way in which the plaintext is processed.** A block cipher process a block at a time and produce an output block for each input block. A stream cipher process the input element continuously, producing output one element at a time, as it goes along.

Cryptanalysis and Brute-Force Attack

- **Cryptanalysis:** Cryptanalytic attacks rely on the nature of the algorithm plus perhaps some knowledge of the general characteristics of the plaintext or even some simple plaintext-ciphertext pairs. This type of attack finds characteristics of the algorithm to find a specific plaintext or to find key.
- **Brute-force attack:** The attacker tries every possible key on a piece of ciphertext until plaintext is obtained. On average, half of all possible keys must be tried to achieve success.
- Based on the amount of information known to the cryptanalyst cryptanalytic attacks can be categorized as:

◦ **Cipher text Only Attack:** The attacker knows only cipher text only. It is easiest to defend.

◦ **Known plaintext Attack:** In this type of attack, the opponent has some plaintext-cipher text pairs. Or the analyst may know that certain plaintext patterns will appear in a message. For example, there may be a standardized header or banner to an electronic funds transfer message and the attacker can use that for generating plaintext-cipher text pairs.

o **Chosen plaintext:** If the analyst is able somehow to get the source system to insert into the system a message chosen by the analyst, then a *chosen-plaintext* attack is possible. In such a case, the analyst will pick patterns that can be expected to reveal the structure of the key.

◦ **Chosen Cipher text:** In this attack, the analyst has cipher text and some plaintext-cipher text pairs where cipher text has been chosen by the analyst.

- **Chosen Text:** Here, the attacker has got cipher text, chosen plaintext-cipher text pairs and chosen cipher text-plaintext pairs.

- Chosen cipher text and chosen text attacks are rarely used.
- It is assumed that the attacker knows the encryption and decryption algorithms.
- Generally, an encryption algorithm is designed to withstand a known-plaintext attack.

Brute-force attack

- This type of attack becomes

impractical as the key size increases as trying all the possible alternative keys for a very large key may take a huge amount of time.

- For example, for a binary key of 128 bits, 2^{128} keys are possible which would require around 5 $X10^{24}$ years at the rate of 1 decryption per microsecond (current machine's speed).

- The Data Encryption Standard (DES) algorithm uses a 56-bit key a 128-bit key is used in AES.
- With massively parallel systems, even DES is also not secure against Brute Force attack.
- AES with its 128-bit key is secure since the time required to break it makes it impractical to try Brute-

Force attack

Substitution Techniques

- Various conventional encryption schemes or substitution techniques are as under:

Caesar cipher

- The encryption rule is simple; replace each letter of the alphabet with the letter standing 3 places further down the alphabet.
- The alphabet is wrapped around so that Z follows A.
- Example:

Plaintext: MEET ME AFTER THE PARTY Ciphertext: PHHW PH DIWHU WKH SDUWB

- Here, the key is 3. If different key is used, different substitution will be obtained.
- Mathematically, starting from a=0, b=1 and so on, Caesar cipher can be written as:

$$E(e) = (e + k) \bmod (26)$$
$$D(C) = (C - k) \bmod (26)$$

- This cipher can be broken

- If we know one plaintext-cipher text pair since the difference will be same.
- By applying Brute Force attack as there are only 26 possible keys.

Monoalphabetic Substitution Cipher

- Instead of shifting alphabets by fixed amount as in Caesar cipher, any random permutation is assigned to the alphabets. This type of encryption is called monoalphabetic substitution cipher.
- For example, A is replaced by Q, B by D, C by T etc. then it will be comparatively stronger than Caesar cipher.
- The number of alternative keys possible now becomes 26!.
- Thus, Brute Force attack is impractical in this case.
- However, another attack is possible. Human languages are redundant i.e. certain characters are used more frequently than others. This fact can be exploited.
- In English 'e' is the most common letter followed by 't', 'r', 'n', 'o', 'a' etc. Letters like 'q', 'x', 'j' are less frequently used.
- Moreover, digrams like 'th' and trigrams like 'the' are also more frequent.
- Tables of frequency of these letters exist. These can be used to guess the plaintext if the plaintext is in uncompressed English language.

Playfair Cipher

- In this technique multiple (2) letters are encrypted at a time.
- This technique uses a 5 X 5 matrix which is also called key matrix.

M
O
N
A
R
C
H
Y
B
D
E
F
G
I/J
K
L
P
Q
S
T
U
V
W
X
Z

- The plaintext is encrypted **two letters at a time**:

  - Break the plaintext into pairs of two consecutive letters.
  - If a pair is a repeated letter, insert a filler like 'X'in the plaintext, eg. "Balloon" is treated as "ba lx lo on".
  - If both letters fall in the same row of the key matrix, replace each with the letter to its right (wrapping back to start from end), eg. "AR" encrypts as "RM".
  - If both letters fall in the same column, replace each with the letter below it (again wrapping to top from bottom), eg. "MU" encrypts to "CM".
  - Otherwise each letter is replaced by the one in its row in the column of the other letter of the pair, eg. "HS" encrypts to "BP", and "EA" to "IM" or "JM" (as desired)

- Security is much improved over monoalphabetic as here two letters are encrypted at a time and hence there are 26 X 26 =676 diagrams and hence it needs a 676 entry frequency table.
- However, it can be broken even if a few hundred letters are known as much of plaintext structure is retained in cipher text.

Hill Cipher

- This cipher is based on linear algebra.
- Each letter is represented by numbers from 0 to 25 and calculations are done m

dulo 26.

- This encryption algorithm takes m successive plaintext letters and substitutes them with m cipher text letters.
- The substitution is determined by m linear equations. For *m* = 3, the system can be described as:

c1 = (k11e1 + k12e2 + k13e3) nod 26 c2 = (k21e1 + k22e2 + k23e3) nod 26 c3 = (k31e1 + k32e2 + k33e3) nod 26

- This can also be expressed in terms of row vectors and matrices.

k11 k12 k13
(c1 c2 c3) = (e1 e2 e3) (k_{21} k_{22} k_{23}) nod 26
k31 k32 k33

Where **C** and **P** are row vectors of length 3 representing the plaintext and cipher text, and **K** is a 3 X 3 matrix representing the encryption key

- Key is an invertible matrix K modulo 26, of size m. For example:

17 17 5 4 19 15

K = (21

18 21) K^{-1} = (15 17 6)
2 2 19 24 0 17

- Encryption and decryption can be given by the following formulae: Encryption: C = PK nod 26

  Decryption: P = CK^{-1} nod 26

- The strength of the Hill cipher is that it completely hides single-letter frequencies.
- Although the Hill cipher is strong against a cipher text-only attack, it is easily broken with a known plaintext attack.

  - Collect m pair of plaintext-cipher text, where m is the size of the key.
  - Write the m plaintexts as the rows of a square matrix P of size m.
  - Write the m cipher texts as the rows of a square matrix C of size m.
  - We have that C=PK mod 26.
  - If P is invertible, then K=P^{-1}C mod 26,
  - If P is not invertible, then collect more plaintext-cipher text pairs until an invertible P is obtained.

The Vigenère cipher

- This is a type of polyalphabetic substitution cipher (includes multiple substitutions depending on the key). In this type of cipher, the key determines which particular substitution is to be used.
- To encrypt a message, a key is needed that is as long as the message. Usually, the key is a repeating keyword.

- For example, if the keyword is *deceptive*, the message "we are discovered save yourself" is encrypted as follows:

  Key: *deceptivedecept*
  Plaintext: wearediscovered Ciphertext:
ZICVTWQNGRZGVTW

- Encryption can be done by looking in the Vigenere Table where ciphertext is the letter key's row and plaintext's column or by the following formula:

  Ci = (Pi + Ki nod n) nod 26

- Decryption is equally simple. The key letter again identifies the row. The position of the cipher text letter in that row determines the column, and the plaintext letter is at the top of that column.
- The strength of this cipher is that there are multiple ciphertext letters for each plaintext letter, one for each unique letter of the keyword.
- Thus, the letter frequency information is obscured however, not all knowledge of the plaintext structure is lost.

Vernam Cipher

- This system works on binary data (bits) rather than letters.
- The technique can be expressed as follows:

$$Ci = Pi \oplus Ki$$

Where
Pi = ith binary digit of plaintext.
Ki = ith binary digit of key.
Ci = ith binary digit of ciphertext.
$\oplus$ = exclusive-or (XOR) operation

- Thus, the ciphertext is generated by performing the bitwise XOR of the plaintext and the key.
- Decryption simply involves the same bitwise operation:

$$Pi = Ci \oplus Ki$$

- The essence of this technique is the means of construction of the key.
- It was produced by the use of a running loop of tape that eventually repeated the key, so that in fact the system worked with a very long but repeating keyword.

- Although such a scheme has cryptanalytic difficulties, but it can be broken with a very long ciphertext or known plaintext as the key is repeated.

One-Time Pad

- In this scheme, a random key that is as long as the message is used.
- The key is used to encrypt and decrypt a single message, and then is discarded. Each new message requires a new key of the same length as the new message.

- This scheme is unbreakable.
- It produces random output that bears no statistical relationship to the plaintext.
- Because the ciphertext contains no information whatsoever about the plaintext, there is simply no way to break the code.
- For any plaintext of equal length to the ciphertext, there is a key that produces that plaintext.

- Therefore, if you did an exhaustive search of all possible keys, you would e plaintexts, with no way of knowing which the intended plaintext was.
- Therefore, the code is unbreakable.
- The security of the one-time pad is entirely due to the randomness of the key.

d up with many legible

- The one-time pad offers complete security but, in practice, has two fundamental difficulties:

    - There is the practical problem of making large quantities of random keys. Any heavily used system might require millions of random characters on a regular basis. Supplying truly random characters in this volume is a significant task.
    - Another problem is that of key distribution and protection. For every message to be sent, a key of equal length is needed by both sender and receiver.

- Because of these difficulties, the one-time pad is used where very high security is required.

- The one-time pad is the only cryptosystem that exhibits **perfect secrecy**.

Transposition Techniques

- A very different kind of mapping is achieved by performing some sort of permutation on the plaintext letters. This technique is referred to as a transposition cipher.
- The simplest such cipher is the **rail fence** technique.

Rail Fence Technique

- Encryption involves writing plaintext letters diagonally over a number of rows, then read off cipher row by row.
- For example, the text “meet me after the party” can be written (in 2 rows) as:

m e m a t r h p r y e t e f e t e o a t

- Ciphertext is read from the above row-by-row: MEMATRHPRYETEFETEAT
- This scheme is very easy to cryptanalyze as no key is involved.
- Transposition cipher can be made significantly more secure by performing more than one stage of transposition. The result is a more complex permutation that is not easily reconstructed.

Difference between Symmetric and Asymmetric key cryptography

Symmetric key Cryptography

Asymmetric Key Cryptography

Symmetric key cryptography uses the same secret (private) key to encrypt and decrypt its data

Asymmetric key cryptography uses a public and a private key to encrypt and decrypt its data

The secret key must be known by both parties.

The public key is known to anyone with which they can encrypt the data but it can only be decoded by the person having the private key

In key distribution process, key information may have to be shared which decreases the security.

Here, the need for sharing key with key distribution center is eliminated.

Symmetric key encryption is faster than asymmetric key.

It is Slower than symmetric key encryption.

Basic operations used in encryption/ decryption are transposition and substitution.

It uses mathematical functions.

Steganography

- Plaintext message may be hidden in one of two ways.
  - Conceal the existence of the message-Steganography.
  - Render the message unintelligible to outsiders by various transformations of the text- Cryptography

- A simple but time consuming form of steganography is the one in which an arrangement of words or letters within an apparently normal text spells out the real message.
- For example, the sequence of first letters of each word of the overall message spells out the hidden message.
- Some other techniques that have been used historically are listed below:

  - **Character marking:** Selected letters of printed or typewritten text are overwritten in pencil. The marks are ordinarily not visible unless the paper is held at an angle to bright light.
  - **Invisible ink:** A number of substances can be used for writing but leave no visible trace until heat or some chemical is applied to the paper.
  - **Pin punctures:** Small pin punctures on selected letters are ordinarily not visible unless the paper is held up in front of a light.

  - **Typewriter correction ribbon:** Used between lines typed with a black typing with the correction tape are visible only under a strong light.

- Although these techniques may seem ancient, they have modern equivalents.

ribbon, the results of

- For example, suppose an image has a resolution of 2048 X 3072 pixels where each pixel is denoted by 24 bits (Kodak CD photo format).

- The least significant bit of each 24-bit pixel can be changed without greatly affecting the quality of the image.
- The result is that you can hide a 2.3-megabyte message in a single digital snapshot.
- There are now a number of software packages available that take this type of approach to steganography.
- Steganography has a number of drawbacks when compared to encryption.

  - It requires a lot of overhead to hide a relatively few bits of information.
  - Once the system is discovered, it becomes virtually worthless.

- The advantage of steganography is that it can be employed by parties who have something to lose if the fact of their secret communication is discovered.

Rotor Machines

- The basic principle of the rotor machine is illustrated in figure. The machine consists of a set of independently rotating cylinders through which electrical pulse can flow.
- Each cylinder has 26 input and 26 output pins, with internal wiring that connect each input pin to unique

output pin.

- If we associate each input and output pin with a letter of the alphabet, then a single cylinder defines a monoalphabetic substitution.
- If we use multiple cylinders then we will obtain polyalphabetic substitution.

CHAPTER TWO

Block Cipher

Block Cipher Principles

Stream Cipher and Block Cipher

- A **stream cipher** is one that encrypts a data stream one bit or one byte at a time. Example of stream cipher are the autokeyes vigenere cipher and vernam cipher.
- A **Block Cipher** is one in which a block of plaintext is treated as a whole and used to produce a cipher text block of equal length. Example of block cipher is DES.

Motivation for the Feistel Cipher Structure

- A block cipher operates on a plaintext block of n bits to produce a ciphertext block of n bits.
- There are 2^n possible different plain text blocks and for the encryption to be reversible each must produce unique ciphertext block.

- Reversible encryption is also called as **singular encryption**. For example singular and non singular transformation for n=2.

Reversible Mapping

Plaintext

Ciphertext

00

11

01

10

10

00

11

01

Text Box: Reversible Mapping Plaintext Ciphertext 00 11 01 10 10 00 11 01

Irreversible Mapping

Plaintext

Ciphertext

00

11

01

10

10

01

11

01

Text Box: Irreversible Mapping Plaintext Ciphertext 00 11 01 10 10 01 11 01

- If we limit ourselves to reversible mapping the number of different transformation is $2^n!$.
- Figure below illustrates the logic of a general substitution cipher for n=4

- A 4-bit input produce one of 16 possible input states, which is mapped by substitution cipher into one of unique 16 possible output states, each of which is represented by 4-bit ciphertext.
- The encryption and decryption mapping can be defined by tabulation, as shown in table. This is the most general form of block cipher and can be used to define any reversible mapping between plaintext and ciphertext.
- Feistel refers to this as the ideal block cipher, because it allows for the maximum number of possible encryption mappings from the plaintext block.

- But there are practical problem with ideal block cipher is if we use small block size such as n=4 then it is vulnerable to statistical analysis of the plain text.
- If n is sufficiently large and an arbitrary reversible substitution between plaintext and ciphertext is allowed then statistical analysis is infeasible.
- Ideal block cipher is not practical for large block size according implementation and performance point of view.
- For such transformation mapping itself is a key and we require $nX2^n$ bits for n bit ideal block cipher which is not practical.
- In considering these difficulties, Feistel points out that what is needed is an approximation to the ideal cipher system for large n, built up out of components that are easily realizable.

The Feistel Cipher

•

Feistel cipher is based on the idea that instead of using Ideal block cipher which degrades performance, a “substitution-permutation network” can be used.

Feistel Cipher Encryption

- The inputs to the encryption algorithm are a plaintext block of length b bits and a key K.

- The plaintext block is divided into two halves.
- The two halves of the data pass through rounds of processing and then combine to produce the ciphertext block.
- Each round has as inputs and derived from the previous round, as well as a subkey derived from the overall K.
- Any number of rounds could be implemented and all rounds have the same structure.
- A **substitution** is performed on the left half of the data. This is done by applying a round function F.
- The Round Function F: F takes right-half block of previous round and a subkey as input.
- The output of the function is XORed with the left half of the data.
- Left and right halves are then swapped.

Feistel Cipher Decryption

- The process of decryption with a Feistel cipher is same as the encryption process.
- The ciphertext is input to the algorithm and the subkeys are used in reverse order. That is, subkey of the last round in encryption is used in the first round in decryption, second last in the second round, and so on.

The exact realization of a Feistel network depends on the choice of the following parameters:

- **Block size**: Larger block sizes mean greater security but reduced encryption/decryption speed for a given algorithm. Traditionally, a block size of 64 bits is used which gives enough security without greatly affecting the speed.
- **Key size:** Larger key size means greater security but may decrease encryption/ decryption speed. The greater security is achieved by greater resistance to brute-force attacks and greater confusion. Key sizes of 64 bits or less are now widely considered to be inadequate, and 128 bits has become a common size.
- **Number of rounds**: The essence of the Feistel cipher is that a single round offers inadequate security but that multiple rounds offer increasing security. A typical size is 16 rounds.

- **Sub key generation algorithm**: Greater complexity in this algorithm leads cryptanalysis.

to greater difficulty of

- **Round function F**: Again, greater complexity generally means greater resistance to cryptanalysis.
- There are two other considerations in the design of a Feistel cipher:
- **Fastsoftwareencryption/decryption**: In many cases, encryption is embedded in applications implementation (as software). Accordingly, the speed of execution of the algorithm becomes a concern.

- **Ease of analysis**: Although we would like to make our algorithm as difficult as possible to crypt analyze, there is great benefit in making the algorithm easy to analyze. That is, if The algorithm can be concisely and clearly explained, it is easier to analyze that algorithm for cryptanalytic vulnerabilities and therefore develop a high level of assurance as to its strength.

The Data Encryption Standard

- SDES encrypts 64-bit blocks using a 56-bit key and produces a 64-bit ciphertext.
- Same steps, with the same key, are used to reverse the encryption with reversed.
- The DES is widely used.

DES Encryption

- The DES encryption is shown in the figure below:

the order of the keys

- Encryption function has two inputs: the plaintext to be encrypted and the key.
- The processing of the plaintext proceeds in three phases.

  - The 64-bit plaintext passes through an initial permutation (IP) that rearranges the bits to produce the permuted input.

- The permuted output is then passed through sixteen rounds of the same function, which involves

both permutation and substitution functions. The left and right halves swapped to produce preoutput.

- The preoutput is passed through a permutation that is the permutation function, to produce the 64-bit cipher text.

from the last round are inverse of the initial

- The right-hand portion of the figure shows the way in which the 56-bit key is used.
  - Initially, the key is passed through a permutation function.
  - Then, a sub key (k_i) is produces for each of the sixteen rounds by the combination of a left circular shift and a permutation.
  - The permutation function is the same for each round, but a different sub key is produced because of the repeated shifts of the key bits.

Initial Permutation (IP) and Inverse Initial Permutation (IP-1)

- The initial permutation and its inverse are defined by tables.
- The tables are to be interpreted as follows.

    - The input to a table consists of 64 bits numbered from 1 to 64.
    - The 64 entries in the permutation table contain a permutation of the numbers from 1 to 64.
    - Each entry in the permutation table indicates the position of a input bit in the output.

- Inverse permutation table nullifies the effect of initial permutation.

Details of Single Round

-

Figure shows the internal structure of a single round.

- The left and right halves are treated as separate 32-bit quantities, labeled L (left) and R (right).
- The overall processing at each round can be summarized as:

$L_i = R_{i-1}$
$R_i = L_{i-1} \oplus F(R_{i-1}, K_i)$
Expansion (E)

- The 32-bit input is first expanded to 48 bits.

- Bits of input are split into groups of 4 bits.
- Each group is written as groups of 6 bits by taking the outer bits from the example

  wo adjacent groups. For

... efgh

ijkl mnop ... is expanded to

m

... defghi hijklm l nopq ...

- The resulting 48 bits are XORed with K_i.

Substitution (S-Box)

- This 48-bit result is input to output.

S-Boxes that perform a substitution on input and produces a 32-bit

-

It is easy to understand S-Box by following figure.

- DES consists of a set of eight S-boxes.

- Each S-Box takes 6 bits as input and produces 4 bits as output.
- The first and last bits of the input to box form a 2-bit binary number which gives the binary value of row number.
- The middle four bits select one of the sixteen columns.
- The decimal value in the cell selected by the row and column is then converted to its 4-bit binary number to produce the output.
- For example, in S1, for input 101110, the row is 10 (row 2) and the column is 0111 (column 7).The value in row 2, column 7 is 11, so the output is 1011.

Permutation (P)

•

The result is again permuted using a permutation table.

Key Generation

- A 64-bit key is used as input to the algorithm while only 56 bits are actually used. Every eighth bit is ignored. Sub-keys at each round are generated as given below:

  - The key is first permuted using a table named Permuted Choice One.
  - The resulting 56-bit key is divided into two 28-bit quantities, C_0 and D_0. At each round, C_{i-1} and D_{i-1} are separately subjected to a circular left shift of 1 or 2 bits, as governed by a table.

o These shifted values are forwarded to the next round. They are also input to a permutation table- Permuted Choice Two.

- The table produces a 48-bit output that serves as the round key k_i.

DES Decryption

- Decryption in DES is same as encryption, except that the sub keys are used in reverse order.

Strength of DES

The Use of 56-Bit Keys

- DES has been developed from LUCIFER which used 128-bit keys.
- As a result, DES with only 56-bit key-length is considered insecure and devices have been proposed time and again showing that DES is no longer secure.

The Nature of the DES

- The only non-linear part of DES is the S-Boxes, design of which was not made public.
- If someone is able to find weakness in S-Box, then attack on DES is possible.
- Characteristics of the algorithm can be exploited as the algorithm is based on linear functions.

Algorithm Timing Attacks

- In this type of attack, the attacker exploits the fact that any algorithm takes different amount of time for different data.

A DES Example

- Let see example of DES and

consider some of its implications. Although you are not expected to

duplicate the example by hand, you will find it informative to study the hex patterns that occure from one step to the next.

Plaintext:

02468aceeca86420

Key:

0f1571c947d9e859

Ciphertext:

Da02ce3a89ecac3b

- **Result:** Above table shows plain text, key and cipher text when we apply all the steps of DES we will get cipher text as shown.

- **The Avalanche Effect:** A desirable property of any encryption algorithm is that a small change in either the plaintext or the key should produce a significant change in cipher text.
- In particular, a change in one bit of plaintext or one bit of the key should produce a change in many bits of the ciphertext. This is referred to as the avalanche effect.
- In DES 1 bit change in input will affect nearly 32 bit of output after all rounds.

Block Cipher Design Principles

- The followed criteria need to be taken into account when designing a block cipher:

- Number f Rounds: The

greater the number of rounds, the more difficult it is to perform

cryptanalysis, even for a weak function. The number of rounds is chosen so that efforts required to crypt analyze it becomes greater than a simple brute-force attack.

- **Design of Function F:** F should be nonlinear and should satisfy strict avalanche criterion (SAC) and bit independence criterion (BIC).

- **S-Box Design:** S-Box obviously should be non-linear and should

satisfy SAC, BIC and

Guaranteed Avalanche criteria. One more obvious characteristic of the S-box is its size. Larger S- Boxes provide good diffusion but also result in greater look-up tables. Hence, general size is 8 to 10.

- **Key Generation Algorithm:** With any Feistel block cipher, the key is used to generate one sub key for each round. In general, sub keys should be selected such that it should be deduce sub keys from one another or main key from the sub key.

Advanced Encryption Standard (AES)

- The more popular and widely

adopted symmetric encryption algorithm likely to be encountered

nowadays is the Advanced Encryption Standard (AES). It is found at least six time faster than triple DES.

- A replacement for DES was needed as its key size was too small. With increasing computing power, it was considered vulnerable against exhaustive key search attack. Triple DES was designed to overcome this drawback but it was found slow.
- The features of AES are as follows

◦ Symmetric key symmetric block cipher

o 128-bit data, 128/192/256-bit keys

◦ Stronger and faster than Triple-DES
◦ Provide full specification and design details
◦ Software implementable in C and Java

AES Structure

- Figure shows the overall structure of the AES encryption process.
- Plain text block size is 128 bits (16 bytes).
- Key size is depends on number of round 128, 192, or 256 bit as shown in table.
- Based on key size AES is named as AES-128, AES-192, or AES-256.
- The input 128 bit block, this block is arranged in the form of 4 X 4 square matrix of bytes. This block is copied into the **state** array, which is modified at each stage of encryption or decryption. After the final stage, State is copied to an output matrix.
- There is a initial single transformation (AddRoundKey) before the first round which can be considered Round 0.
- The first N-1 rounds consist of four distinct transformation function: SubBytes, ShiftRows, MixColumns, and AddRoundKey,which are described subsequently.
- The final round contains only first three transformations of above round.

- Each transformation takes one or more 4 X 4 matrices as input and produces a 4 X 4 matrix as output.
- The key expansion function generates N+1 round key each of which is distinct 4 X 4 matrices. Each round key serves as one of the inputs to the AddRoundKey transformation in each round.

Detail Structure

- Figure shows detail encryption Decryption process of AES.
- Lets discuss Several comments about AES structure:

1. It is not a Feistel structure. As we know in feistel structure half of the data block is used to modify the other half of the data block and then the halves are swapped. While in AES we use full data block as a single matrix during each round.
2. The key is expanded into an array of fourty-four 32-bit words. And such four word (128-bit) serves as round key for each round.
3. Four different stages are used one of permutation and three of substitution:

    - **SubBytes**: Uses an S-box to perform a byte-by-byte substitution of the block.
    - **ShiftRows**: A simple permutation.

    - **MixColumns**: A substitution that makes use of arithmetic over bytes.
    - **AddRoundKey**: A simple bitwise XOR of the current block with a portion of the expanded key.

2. The structure is quite simple for both encryption and decryption it begins with AddRoundKey, followed by nine rounds of all four stages, followed by tenth round of three stages.

3. Only AddRoundKey stage use key for this reason, the cipher begins and ends with an AddRoundKey stage. Any other stage, applied at the beginning or end, is reversible without knowledge of the key and so would add no security.
4. The AddRoundKey stage is in effect, a form of Vernam cipher and by itself would not be formidable. The other three stages together provide confusion, diffusion, and nonlinearity, but by themselves would provide no security because they do not use the key.
5. Each stage is easily reversible.
6. In AES decryption algorithm is not identical to encryption algorithm.
7. Once it is established that all four stages are reversible, it is easy to verify that decryption does recover the plain text.
8. For making AES reversible the final round of both encryption and decryption are consists of only three stages.

AES Transformation Function

Substitute bytes Transformation (Forward & Inverse)

- Substitute bytes transformation is simple table lookup. There is separate table for forward and inverse operation.
- 16 X 16 matrix of byte value called s-box that contains the permutation of all 256 8-bit values. Each individual

byte of state is mapped into a new byte in the following way.

- The left most 4-bit of the byte are used as row number and right most 4-bit are used as column number. Now row and column number serves as index into the s-box to select unique 8-bit output value.

AES S-Box

- For example hexadecimal value 68 is referred to row 6 and column 8 and value in table at that position is 45 so byte value 68 is replaced with 45.
- For inverse substitute byte procedure is same but S-box is different. Reverse of above example is shown in figure.

AES Inverse S-Box

- S-box is constructed in the following fashion:

Byte at row y, column x initialized to yx

yx

Text

Box: yx

Inverse in GF (2^8)

Byte at row y, column x initialized to yx

yx

Text

Box: yx

Byte to bit column vector

Byte to bit

bO, 0

1 bO 1

column vector

Fb1,1 F1

Ib ,I I0

0 1 Fb11

1 I Ib I

F01

I1I

I

I 2 I

0

1

0

0

1

0

0

0

1

0

0

1

1

0

0

1

0

0

,

I I 2I I I

I1

0

1

0

0

1

0

I0

1

0

1

0

0

1

I0

0

1

0

1

0

0

I

0

0

1

0

1

0

L0

1

0

0

1

0

1

Ib3,I =

0 I Ib3I + I0I

1

1

bO,

F ,1

1 0 0 0 1 1 1

F

11 F

bO1 1

Ib4 I

Ib ,I

0. I Ib4I
1. I Ib I

I0I

I0I

Ib1 I

1 1 0 0 0 1 1 Ib I

F11

I 5,I

I I 5I I I

Ib2,I

I1 1 1 0 0 0 1

1I Ib2I

I0I

Ib6 I 1

Ib6I 0

Bit column vector to yte

Inverse in

GF (2^8)

IS(yx)

Ib ·I I

I Ib I I I

Lb7,l

l Lb7l

L0l

I 3,I = I1 1 1 1 0 0 0 1I

3 + I0I

6

Ib4,I Ib5,I

Ib I

I1 1 1 1 1 1 0 0

I0 1 1 1 1 1 1 0

I0 0 1 1 1 1 1 1

0I Ib4I

0I Ib_5I

I

6I

0I Ib I

I0I I1I I1I

Lb7,l

L0 0 0 1 1 1 1

1l Lb7l

L0l

Bit column
vector to byte

S(yx)

a.

e

Calculation of bytat

b. **Calculation**

of byte at

row y, column x of S-boxrow y, column x of IS-

- Construction of S-box:

1. Initialize the S-box with the byte values in ascending sequence row by row.
2. Map each byte in the S-box to its multiplicative inverse in the finite field GF (2^8). The value {00} is mapped to itself.
3. Consider that each byte in the S-box consist of 8 bits labeled (b_7, b_6, b_5, b_4, b_3, b_2, b_1, b_0). Apply the transformation using matrix multiplication as shown in figure.
4. Finally convert that bit column vector to byte.

- Construction of IS-box:

1. Initialize the IS-box with the byte values in ascending sequence row by row.
2. Consider that each byte in the IS-box consist of 8 bits labeled (b_7, b_6, b_5, b_4, b_3, b_2, b_1, b_0). Apply the transformation using matrix multiplication as shown in figure.
3. Convert that bit column vector to byte.
4. Map each byte in the IS-box to its multiplicative inverse in the finite field GF (2^8).

ShiftRows Transformation (Forward & Inverse)

- The **forward shift row transformation** is performed as below:

1. The first row of state is not altered.
2. In second row we apply 1-byte circular left shift.
3. In third row we apply 2-byte circular left shift.
4. In fourth row we apply 3-byte circular left shift.

- In the **inverse shift row transformation** we apply right circular rotation.

1. The first row of state is not altered.
2. In second row we apply 1-byte circular right shift.
3. In third row we apply 2-byte circular right shift.
4. In fourth row we apply 3-byte circular right shift.

MixColumns Transformation (Forward & Inverse)

- In the forward MixColumn transformation each byte of a column is mapped into a new value that is a function of all bytes in that column.

- The transformation can be defined by the following matrix multiplication on state:

02 03 01
01 02 03
01 SO,O SO,1 SO,2 SO,3
01 FS1,O S1,1 S1,2 S1,31
SO,O, SO,1, SO,2, SO,3,
FS1,O, S1,1, S1,2, S1,3,1
[ ] I

I = I ,

, , ,I
01 01 02
03 01 01
03 IS2,O S2,1 S2,2 S2,3I
02 LS3,O S3,1 S3,2 S3,3l
IS2,O S2,1 S2,2 S2,3 I LS3,O, S3,1, S3,2, S3,3,l

- In this case, the individual additions and multiplications are performed in GF (2^8).
- In the inverse MixColumn transformation procedure is same but matrix is different which is shown below.

0E 0B 0D
09 0E 0B
09 SO,O SO,1 SO,2 SO,3
0D FS1,O S1,1 S1,2 S1,31
SO,O, SO,1, SO,2, SO,3,
FS1,O, S1,1, S1,2, S1,3,1
[ ] I
I = I , ,
, ,I

0D 09 0E
0B 0D 09
0B IS2,O S2,1 S2,2 S2,3I
0E LS3,O S3,1 S3,2 S3,3l
IS2,O S2,1 S2,2 S2,3 I LS3,O, S3,1, S3,2, S3,3,l

AddRoundKey Transformation

- In this transformation 128 bits state are bitwise XORed with the 128 bits of the round key.
- It is viewed as a byte level operation.

-

Example

- Inverse of AddRoundKey is same because inverse of XOR is again XOR.

AES Key Expansion

- AES takes 16-byte key as input.
- g

S
S
S
S
W’
w

B_0

B_1

B_2

B_3

As shown in figure below key expansion process is straight forward.

K_0

K_4

K_8

K12

K_1

K_5

K_9

K13

K_2

K_6

K10

K14

K_3

K_7

K11

K15

w_0

w_1

w_2

w

w_0

w_1

w_2

w

RC_j

0

0

0

b.

3

Function g.

W40

w41

w42

W43

3

B_1

B_2

B_3

B_0

B_1'

B_2'

B_3'

B_0'

a.

a

Overall Key expansion lgorithm.

- First of all key is stores in 4X4 matrix in column major matrix as shown in figure.

- Each column combines to form 32 bit word.
- Than we apply function g to every fourth word that is w3, w7, w11 etc.

- Than X-OR operation is performed as shown in figure to obtain next four word. And this process continues till generation of all words.
- As shown in figure (b) internal structure of function g.
- First we convert word to 4 byte.
- Then apply circular left shift operation.
- Then apply substitute byte operation using S-box which is same as S-box of AES encryption process.
- Than we apply X-OR operation with round constant which have least significant 3 byte as zero and most significant byte is depend on round number which is shown in table below.

Round (j)

1

2

3

4

5

6

7

8

9

10

RC[j]

01

02

04

08

10
20
40
80
1B
36

- And output of this function is used for X-OR operation as shown in figure (a).

AES Example

- Let see example of AES and consider some of its implications.
- Although you are not expected to duplicate the example by hand, you will find it informative to study the hex patterns that occur from one step to the next.

Plaintext:
0123456789abcdeffedcba9876543210
Key:
0f1571c947d9e8590cb7add6af7f6798
Ciphertext:
Ff0b844a0853bf7c6934ab4364148fb9

- **Result:** Above table shows plain text, key and cipher text when we apply all the steps of AES we will get cipher text as shown.
- **The Avalanche Effect:** A desirable property of any encryption algorithm is that a small change in either the plaintext or the key should produce a significant change

in cipher text.

- In particular, a change in one bit of plaintext or one bit of the key should produce a change in many bits of the ciphertext. This is referred to as the avalanche effect.
- In AES 1 bit change in input will affect nearly all bit of output after all rounds.

AES Implementation

Equivalent Inverse Cipher

- While implementing AES if we interchange the order of operation than it will affect the result or not is discussed here.
- If we interchange inverse shift row and inverse substitute byte operation than it will not affect and we get the same output.
- So we can obtain two equivalent decryption algorithms for one encryption algorithm.
- As inverse shift row will change position of byte and it will not affect byte value. While inverse substitute byte will change byte value by table lookup and it not concern with byte position. So we can interchange those two operations.
- If we interchange inverse mix column and add round key operation than it will affect and we do not get the same output.
- Both the operation will affect the value and so it cannot be interchange.

Implementation Aspects

- As in AES out of four three operation are byte level operation and it can be efficiently implemented on 8- bit processors.

- Only mix column operation is requiring matrix multiplication which requires some storage space and also time consuming on 8-bit processor.
- To overcome it we can use table lookup to reduce time requirement.
- Also we can implement it on 32-bit processors.
- In 32-bit processor we can use word by word operation and it much faster.

CHAPTER THREE

Multiple Encryption

Multiple Encryption and Triple DES

- As we know that DES is venerable to brute-force attack, we are interested to find an alternative.
- One possible solution is to design completely new algorithm like AES.
- Second solution is to use DES multiple times.

Double DES

- The simplest form of multiple encryptions has two encryption stages and two keys and is known as Double DES.

- Given a plaintext P and two encryption keys K1 and K2, cipher text C is generated as: **C = E(K2, E(K1, P))**
- Decryption applies keys in reverse order: **P = D(K1, D(K2, C))**
- This scheme involves a key length of 56 * 2 = 112 bits, making Brute-Force attack impractical.
- However, other types of attacks are possible:

Reduction to a Single Stage

- If it is possible to find a key such that: **E(K2, E(K1, P)) = E(K3, P)** then double encryption, or any number of stages of multiple encryption with DES, would be useless.
- Because the result would be equivalent to a single encryption with a single 56- bit key.
- However, by the principle of reverse mapping, such a key is not possible.

Meet-In-The-Middle Attack

- This attack is based on the on the observation that if:

  $C = E(K_2, E(K_1, P))$, **then**
  $X = E(K_1, P) = D(K_2, C)$

- Given a known (P, C) pair, the attack proceeds as follows:

  - First, encrypt P for all 256 possible values of K1.
  - Store these results in a table and then sort the table by the values of X.
  - Decrypt C using all 256 possible values of K2.
  - Check the result against the table for a match after every decryption.
  - If a match occurs, then test the two resulting keys against a new known plaintext– ciphertext pair.
  - If the two keys produce the correct ciphertext, accept them as the correct keys.
  - For any given plaintext, 248 false alarms are possible since there are only 264 ciphertext values whereas 2112 key values.
  - Thus, the order of attack can be reduced to 248 instead of 2112.

Triple DES with Two Keys

- An alternative to the meet-in-the-middle attack is to use three stages of encryption with three or two different keys.

- The function follows an encrypt decrypt-encrypt (EDE) sequence.

  $C = \mathrm{E}(K1, \mathrm{D}(K2, \mathrm{E}(K1, P)))$
  $P = \mathrm{D}(K1, \mathrm{E}(K2, \mathrm{D}(K1, C)))$

- 3DES with two keys is a relatively popular alternative to DES.
- Currently, there are no practical cryptanalytic attacks on 3DES.
- Brute-force key search on 3DES is on the order of 2112 and the cost of differential cryptanalysis also has an exponential growth, compared to single DES.
- Several proposed attacks (though impractical) on 3DES are:

Chosen-Plaintext Attack

- Find plaintext values that gives A = 0.
- Then, use the meet-in-the- middle attack to determine the two keys.
- However, this attack requires 256 chosen plaintext-cipher text pairs which is impractical.

Known-Plaintext Attack

- This method does not require chosen plaintext-cipher text pairs but requires more effort.
- The attack is based on the observation that if an attacker knows A and C, then the problem reduces to that of an attack on double DES.
- The attack is as follows:
    - The attacker obtains n(P, C) pairs places them in Table 1 sorted on the values of P.
    - For an arbitrary value a for A, calculate the plaintext value that produces: Pi = D(i, a)
    - For each Pi that matches an entry in Table 1, create an entry in Table 2 that contains value of K1 and b that is obtained by decrypting the corresponding cipher text from Table 2.

B = D(i, C)

- Table 2 contains a number of candidate values of Ki. Now, for each of the 256 possible values of K2, calculate the second intermediate value for our chosen value of a:

Bj = D(j, a)

- At each step, look up Bj in Table 2. If there is a match, then the corresponding key i from Table 2 plus this value of j are candidate values for the unknown keys (K1, K2).
- Test each candidate pair of keys on a few other plaintext–cipher text pairs. If a pair of keys produces the desired cipher text, the task is complete.
- If no pair succeeds, repeat from step 1 with a new value of a.

Triple DES with Three Keys

- Although the attacks just described appear impractical, anyone using two-key 3DES may feel some concern.
- In that case, three-key 3DES is the preferred alternative.

- Three-key 3DES has an effective key length of 168 bits and is defined as: C = E(K3, D(K2, E(K1, P)))
- Backward compatibility with DES is provided by putting K3 = K1 or K1 = K3.
- A number of Internet-based applications have adopted three-key 3DES, including PGP and S/MIME.

Modes of Operations

There are 5 modes of operation which are listed below.

1. Electronic Codebook mode (ECB)

- This is the simplest mode in which plaintext is handled one block at a time and each block of plaintext is encrypted using the same key.

- The term codebook is used because, for a given key, there is a unique ciphertext for every -bit block of plaintext.
- Therefore, we can imagine a huge codebook in which there is an entry for every possible b-bit plaintext

showing its corresponding ciphertext.

- For a message longer than b bits, the procedure is simply to break the message into b-bit blocks, padding the last block if necessary.
- Decryption is performed one block at a time, always using the same key.
- For lengthy messages, ECB mode may be not secure. If the message has repetitive elements, then these elements can be identified by the analyst.
- Thus, the ECB method is ideal for a short amount of data, such as an encryption key.

1.

Cipher Block Chaining Mode (CBC)

- To overcome the security deficiencies of ECB, a technique is needed in which the same plaintext block, if repeated, produces different cipher text blocks.
- A simple way to satisfy this requirement is the cipher block chaining (CBC) which is shown in the figure.
- In this mode, the input to the encryption algorithm is the X-OR of the current plaintext block and the

preceding ciphertext block; the same key is

- used for each block.
- The input to the encryption function for each plaintext block has no fixed relationship to the plaintext block.
- Therefore, repeating patterns will not produce same ciphertext.
- The last block is padded to a full b bits if it is a partial block.
- For decryption, each cipher block is passed through the decryption algorithm. The result is X-ORed with the preceding ciphertext block to produce the plaintext block.
- The expressions for CBC are:

Encryption:
Cj = E(K, [Cj — 1 ⊕ Pj)
Decryption:
D(K, Cj) = D(K, E(K, [cj — 1 ⊕ Pj])) D(K, Cj) = Cj — 1 ⊕ Pj
Cj — 1 ⊕ D(K, Cj) = Cj — 1 ⊕ Cj — 1 ⊕ Pj = Pj

3. Cipher Feedback Mode (CFB)

- DES is a block cipher, but it may be used as a stream cipher if the Cipher Fee Output Feedback Mode (OFB) is used. CFB scheme is depicted below.

  back Mode (CFB) or the

- A stream cipher eliminates the need to pad a message to be an integral number of blocks.
- It also can operate in real time.

- **'s'** bits is the size usually selected by the user, most of time it is 8 bits.
- In this case, rather than block of 64 bits, the plaintext is divided into segments of s bits.
- **Encryption:** The input to the encryption function is a 64-bit shift register that is initially set to some initialization vector (IV).
- The leftmost (most significant) s bits of the output of the encryption function are X-ORed with the first segment of plaintext P1 to produce the first unit of ciphertext C1, which is then transmitted.
- In addition, the contents of the shift register are shifted left by s bits and C1 is placed in the rightmost

  s bits of the shift register.

- This process continues until all plaintext units have been encrypted.
- **Decryption:** The same scheme is used except that the received ciphertext unit is X-ORed with the output of the encryption function to produce the plaintext unit.
- The disadvantage of this scheme is that bit error in one ciphertext propagates to next stage also.

4.

Output Feedback Mode (OFB)

- The Output Feedback Mode (OFB) is similar in structure to that of CFB:
- The difference between CFB and OFB is that in OFB the output of the encryption function is fed back to the shift register in OFB, whereas in CFB the ciphertext is fed to the shift register.
- The other difference is that the OFB mode operates on full blocks of plaintext and ciphertext, not on ‘s’ bit subset.
- One advantage of the OFB method is that bit errors in transmission do not propagate.
- The disadvantage of OFB is that it is more vulnerable to a message stream modification attack than CFB.

5.

Counter Mode (CTR)

- In this mode, a counter equal to the plaintext block size is used.
- The only requirement is that encrypted.

the counter value must be different for each

plaintext block that is

- Typically, the counter is initialized to some value and then incremented by 1 for each subsequent block (modulo 2^b, where **b** is the block size)
- Counter Mode works as follows:
- **Encryption**: The counter is encrypted and then X-ORed with the plaintext block to produce the cipher text block; there is no chaining.
- **Decryption**: The same sequence of counter values is used. Each encrypted counter is X-ORed with a cipher text block to recover the corresponding plaintext block.
- CTR has following advantages:

    - **Hardware efficiency:** In this mode, encryption (or decryption) can be done in parallel on multiple blocks of plaintext or cipher text. For the chaining modes, the algorithm must complete the computation on one block before beginning on the next block.
    - **Software efficiency:** Similarly, because of the opportunities for parallel execution in CTR mode, processors that support parallel features, such as aggressive pipelining, multiple instruction dispatch per clock cycle, large number of registers can be effectively utilized.
    - **Preprocessing:** The execution of the encryption algorithm does not depend on input of the plaintext or cipher text. Therefore preprocessing can be used to prepare the output of the encryption boxes which can be fed into the X-OR functions when the plaintext or cipher text input is presented.

- **Random access:** The i^{th}block of plaintext or cipher text can be processed in random-access fashion. With the chaining modes, block cannot be computed until **i– 1** prior block is computed.
- **Provable security:** It can be shown that CTR is as secure as the other modes.
- **Simplicity:** CTR mode requires only the implementation of the encryption algorithm and not the decryption algorithm and has a very simple implementation.

- This mode is used in ATM (asynchronous transfer mode) and IPsec (IP security) nowadays.

CHAPTER FOUR

Public Key Cryptography

Define Public Key Cryptography

Public-key cryptography is a cryptographic system that uses two separate keys, one of which is secret and

the other one is public. The algorithms used for public key cryptography are functions.

Public Key Cryptosystem

based on mathematical

- A public-key encryption scheme has six parts.

    - **Plaintext:** This is the readable message or data that is fed into the algorithm as input.
    - **Encryption algorithm:** The encryption algorithm performs various transformations on the plaintext.
    - **Public and private keys:** This is a pair of keys that have been selected so that if one is used for encryption, the other is used for decryption.
    - **Ciphertext:** This is the scrambled message produced as output. It depends on the plaintext and the key

    - **Decryption algorithm:** This algorithm accepts the ciphertext and the matching key and produces the original plaintext.

- Any cryptosystem are designed to meet following goal

  1. Secrecy (Encryption)
  2. Authentication

- Now we will discuss how it is maintain in public key cryptosystem

Public Key Cryptosystem: Secrecy

Encryption using public key cryptography

- The essential steps are the following.
  - Each user generates a pair of keys to be used for the encryption and decryption of messages.
  - Each user places one of the two keys in a public register or other accessible file. This is the public key. The other key is kept private.
  - If A wishes to send a confidential message to B, A encrypts the message using B's public key.
  - When B receives the message, it decrypts it using the private key. No other recipient can decrypt the message because only B knows B's private key.
  - As long as a user's private key remains protected and secret, incoming communication is secure.
  - At any time, a system can change its private key and publish the companion public key to replace its old public key.

- Suppose there is some source A that produces a message in plaintext, $X = [X_1, X_2, \ldots, X_M]$ and sends it to B.
- B generates a related pair of keys: a public key, PU_b, and a private key, PR_b. $PU_b$is publicly available and therefore accessible by A.
- With the message X and the encryption key PU_b as input, A forms the ciphertext $Y = [Y_1, Y_2, \ldots, Y_N]$:

$$Y = E(PU_b, X)$$

- The intended receiver, having the matching private key, is able to decrypt the message:

$$X = D\ (PR_b, Y)$$

- An adversary, observing Y and having access to Pu_b only, may attempt to recover X and/or PR_b.

- If the adversary is interested only in this particular message, then the focus of effort is to recover X by generating a plaintext estimate.
- Whereas if the adversary is interested in being able to read future messages as well, then he attempts to recover PR_b by generating an estimate

Public Key Cryptosystem: Authentication

Authentication using public key cryptography

- However, the above scheme does not provide authentication of sender as, anyone having access to the public key can encrypt the message.
- Public-key encryption can be used to provide authentication in the following manner:
    - When A wishes to send a message to B where confidentiality is not needed but authentication is

required, A encrypts the message using PR_a.

  - Anyone having access to PU_a can decrypt the message. However, one thing is sure that the message originated from A since no one except A could have encrypted the message using PR_a.

- A prepares a message to B and encrypts it using A's private key before transmitting it.

$$Y = E\ (PRa, X)$$

- B can decrypt the message using A's public key.

$$X = D\ (PUa, Y)$$

- Because the message was encrypted using A's private key, only A could have prepared the message. Therefore, the entire encrypted message serves as a digital signature.
- In addition, it is impossible to alter the message without access to A's private key, so the message is authenticated both in terms of source and in terms of data integrity.
- However, the entire message needs to be stored to bring up in case of dispute.
- A more efficient way of achieving the same results is to encrypt a small block of bits that is a function of the document.
- Such a block, called an authenticator.

- It must have the property that it is infeasible to change the document authenticator.

without changing the

- If the authenticator is encrypted with the sender's private key, it serves as a signature.

Public Key Cryptosystem: Authentication and Secrecy

- Authentication and Secrecy both can be achieved by combining above both techniques.
    - First sender A encrypt message X with private key of A.

$$Y = E(PRa, X)$$

- Then again A encrypt Y with public key of B.
- Then send Z.

$Z = E(PUb, Y)$

- Only B can decrypt Z as it is encrypted with public key of B. So it gives Secrecy.

$$Y = D(PRb, Z)$$

- Now Y can be decrypted with public key of A. So it gives authentication.

$$X = D(PUa, Y)$$

- So by using public key cryptography we can achieve secrecy and authentication.

Applications of Public Key Cryptography

- Applications of public-key cryptosystems can classified into three categories:

1. **Encryption/decryption:** The sender encrypts a message with the recipient's public key.
2. **Digital signature:** The sender "signs" a message with its private key. Signing is achieved by a cryptographic algorithm applied to the message or to a small block of

data that is a function of the message.

1. **Key exchange:** Two sides possible.

cooperate to exchange a session key. Several different methods are

- Some algorithm like RSA and Elliptic Curve are suitable for all three applications whereas others can be used for one or two of these applications.

Requirements for Public Key Cryptography

- Requirements that public key algorithms must fulfill are:
    - It is computationally easy for a party B to generate a key pair.
    - It is computationally easy for a sender A, knowing the public key and themessage **M**, to generate the corresponding ciphertext and for the receiver B to decrypt the resulting ciphertextusing the private key to recover the original message.
    - It is computationally infeasible for an adversary, knowing the public key, $\mathbf{PU_b}$, todetermine the private key,$\mathbf{PR_b}$.
    - It is computationally infeasible for an adversary, knowing the public key, $\mathbf{PU_b}$, and a ciphertext, **C**, to recover the original message, **M.**
    - The two keys can be applied in either order:

$$M = D[PU_b, E(PR_b,M)] = D[PR_b, E(PU_b,M)]$$

- These are requirements that only a few algorithms have been able to fulfill. Some of these are RSA, elliptic curve cryptography, Diffie-Hellman, & DSS.

Public Key Cryptanalysis

Brute force attack

- This attack includes trying all the alternate keys until the correct key is found.
- Counter measure to this is use large keys.
- However, public-key systems depend on the use of some sort of invertible mathematical function which is really time-consuming and increases overhead.
- Thus, there is a tradeoff. The key size must be large enough to make brute-force attack impractical but small enough for practical encryption and decryption.
- Secure keys are long enough to make encryption decryption really slow.
- Hence, public-key encryption is currently confined to key management and signature applications

Computation of private key from public key

- In this attack, some characteristics of algorithm are exploited to calculate the private key from public key.
- This attack needs many known or chosen plaintext-ciphertext pairs.
- To date it has not been mathematically proven that this form of attack is infeasible for a particular algorithm. Thus any given algorithm is suspect.

Probable message attack

- In this attack, the opponent has some idea about the plaintext and he uses this information to find the private key.
- Suppose that a message consist only a 56-bit DES key.
- An adversary could encrypt all possible 56-bit DES keys using the public key and could discover the encrypted key by matching the transmitted ciphertext.
- Thus, no matter how large the key size of the public-key scheme, the attack is reduced to a brute-force attack on a 56-bitkey.
- This attack can be prevented by appending some random bits to such simple messages.

The RSA Algorithm

- RSA algorithm processes plaintext blocks, with each block having a binary value less than some number n.
- The block size must be less than or equal to $\log_2(n) + 1$.
- Steps for RSA:

- Select two large prime numbers **p** and **q.**
- Calculate n = pq.
- Calculate $\phi(n) = (p - 1)(q - 1)$.
- Select e such that e is relatively prime to $\phi(n)$.
- Compute d such that $d*e \equiv 1 \pmod{\phi(n)}$.

- RSA is a public key algorithm with public key PU = {e, n} and private key PR = {d, n}.
- Encryption and decryption are of the following form, forsome plaintext block M and ciphertext block C:

$$C = M^e mod\ n\ M = C^d mod\ n$$

M= $(M^e)^d$ mod n

- For the above equation to be true, d must be an inverse of e.
- D can be calculated from e using extended Euclid's algorithm.
- Both sender and receiver must know the value of n.
- The sender knows the value of e, and only the receiver knows the value of d.
- RSA can also be subjected to various attacks like brute-force attack, various mathematical attacks, timing attacks and chosen ciphertext attacks.
- Some of these attacks exploit the mathematical characteristics of RSA.

RSA Example

- Let p = 17 and q = 11.

- $n = pq = 17 X 11 = 187$
- $\phi(n) = (p-1)(q-1) = 16 X 10 = 160$
- Let e be 7.
- $d = e^{-1} \bmod 160 = 23$ (can be calculated by extended Euclid's algorithm).
- Now, PU = { 7, 187 } and PR = { 23, 187 }
- If M = 88, then by RSA

Encryption

$C = 88^7 \bmod 187$
$= [\ 88 X 88^2 X 88^4\ ] \bmod 187$
$= 11$

Decryption

- Here, C = 11.

$M = 11^{23} \bmod 187$
$= [\ 11 X 11^2 X 11^4 X 11^8 X 11^8\ ] \bmod 187$
$= 88$

Computational Aspects of RSA

- Use of modular arithmetic makes calculation practical:
    - Both encryption and decryption in RSA involve calculating huge exponents, mod n.

- If the exponentiation is done over the integers and then reduced modulo n, the intermediate values would be extremely large.
- However, the following property of modular arithmetic makes the calculation practical:

$$[(a \bmod n) * (b \bmod n)] \bmod n = (a * b) \bmod n]$$

- **Efficiency of exponentiation:**
  - RSA deals with very large exponents.
  - But this operation can be implemented efficiently.
  - Consider x^{16}. A straightforward approach requires multiplying x 16 times.
  - But, the same can be achieved by only four multiplications - x^2,$(x^2)^2=x^4$, $(x^4)^2=x^8$, $(x^8)^2=x^{16}$.
- Efficient operation using the public key:
  - To speed up the operation of the RSA algorithm using the public key, a specific choice of e is usually made.
  - The most common choice is 65537 ($2^{16} + 1$).

The Security of RSA

Four possible approaches to attacking the RSA algorithm are

Brute force

- This involves trying all possible private keys.
- The defense against this attack is to use a large key.
- However, the key should not be so large that it makes calculation too time consuming and hence impractical.
- Thus, there is a tradeoff between key size and security of RSA.

Mathematical attacks

- There are three approaches to attacking RSA mathematically, all of which are equivalent in effort to the factoring the product of two primes.
    - Factor n into its two prime factors. This enables calculation of f(n) = (p - 1)(q - 1), which in turn enables determination of d $=e^{-1}$ (mod f(n)).
    - Determine f(n) directly, without first determining p and q. Again, this enables determination of d $=e^{-1}$ (mod f(n)). This is equivalent to factoring n.
    - Determine d directly, without first determining f(n) which is at least as time-consuming as the factoring problem.
- Size of **n** should be considerably large.
- To avoid values of **n** that may be factored more easily, the
    - **P** and **q** should differ in length by only a few digits.

- Both (p - 1) and (q - 1) should contain a large prime factor.
- gcd(p - 1, q - 1) should be small.

Timing attacks

- These depend on the running time of the decryption algorithm.
- It is a ciphertext only attack.
- In RSA, modular exponentiation is done bit by bit. Suppose the system uses a modular multiplication function that is very fast in almost all cases but in a few cases takes much more time than an entire average modular exponentiation.
- The attack proceeds as follows:
  - Suppose that the first j bits are known.
  - For a given ciphertext, the attacker can complete the first j iterations of the for-loop.
  - The operationof the subsequent step depends on the unknown exponent bit.

  - For a few values of e and d, the modular multiplication will be extremely slow, and the attacker knows which these are.

  - Therefore, if the observed

time to execute the decryption algorithm is
always slow when this

particular iteration is slow with a 1 bit, then this bit is assumed to be 1.

 - If a number of observed execution times for the entire algorithm are fast, then this bit is assumed to be 0.

- Generally modular exponentiation implementations do not have such extreme timing variations but there is enough variation to make this attack practical.
- Countermeasures to this attack are:

 - **Constant exponentiation time:** Ensure that all exponentiations take the before returning a result. However, this degrades performance.
 - **Random delay:** Better performance could be achieved by adding a

same amount of time

random delay to the

exponentiation algorithm to confuse the timing attack. But if the defenders don't add enough noise, attackers could still succeed by additional measurements to compensate for the random delays.

 - **Blinding:** Multiply the ciphertext by a random number before performing exponentiation. This process prevents the attacker from knowing what ciphertext bits are being processed inside the computer and therefore prevents the bit-by-bit analysis that is essential to the timing attack. Steps for blinding are:

- Generate a secret random number **r** between 0 and n – 1.
- **$C' = C(r^e)$ mod n**, where e is the public exponent.
- Compute **$M' = (C')^d$mod n**
- Compute **$M = M'r^{-1}$ mod n**, r^{-1} is the multiplicative inverse of r mod n

Implementing blinding incurs only a 2 to 10% performance penalty.

Chosen ciphertext attacks

- This type of attack exploits properties of the RSA algorithm.
- The adversary could select a plaintext, encrypt it with the target's public key, and then gets the plaintext back by having it decrypted with the private key.
- This provides no new information. Instead, the adversary exploits properties of RSA and selects blocks of data that, when processed using the target's private key, gives information needed for cryptanalysis.
- An example of one such attack is that the attacker exploits the following property of RSA.

$$E(PU,M1)\times E(PU,M2) = E(PU, [M1 \times M2])$$

  - Compute $X = (C\times 2^e) \bmod n$.
  - Submit X as a chosen ciphertext and receive back $Y = X^d \bmod n$

- But now note that

$$X = (C \bmod n) * (2^e \bmod n)$$

= (M^e mod n) * (2^emod n)

X = $(2M)^e$ mod n

- Therefore, Y = (2M) mod n.

- To overcome this simple attack, randomly pad the plaintext before encryption.
- This randomizes the ciphertext so that the Equation no longer holds.

Diffie-Hellman key exchange

- The purpose of the algorithm is to enable two users to securely exchange a key that can be used for encryption of messages.

- The Diffie-Hellman algorithm depends on the difficulty of computing discrete logarithms.
- For this scheme, there are two publicly known numbers: a prime number **q** and an integer **α** that is a primitive root of **q.**
- Suppose the users A and B wish to exchange a key.
- User A selects a random private integer $X_A < q$ and computes public integer

$$Y_A = \alpha^{XA} \bmod q.$$

- Similarly, user B independently selects a random private integer $X_B < q$ and computes public integer

$$Y_B = \alpha^{XB} \bmod q.$$

- Each side keeps the **X** value private and makes the **Y** value available publicly to the other side.
- User A computes the key as

$$K = (Y_B)^{XA} \bmod q \text{ and}$$

- User B computes the key as

$$K = (Y_A)^{XB} \bmod q.$$

- These two calculations produce identical results:

$$K = (Y_A)^{XB} mod q$$

$$= (\alpha^{XA} \bmod q)^{XB} mod q$$
$$= (\alpha^{XA})^{XB} mod q$$

= α^{XBXA}**mod q**

= $(\alpha^{XB})^{XA}$**mod q** (by the rules of modular arithmetic)

$$= (\alpha^{XB} mod q)^{XA} mod\ q$$

= $(Y_B)^{XA}$**mod q**

- The result is that the two sides have exchanged a secret value.
- Furthermore, because $X_A$and $X_B$are private, an adversary only has the following information: q, α, Y_A and Y_B.
- Thus, the adversary is forced to take a discrete logarithm to determine the key.
- For example, to determine the private key of user B, an adversary must compute

$$X_B = dlog_{a,q}(Y_B)$$

- The adversary can then calculate the key K.
- The security of the Diffie-Hellman key exchange lies in the fact that, while it is relatively easy to calculate exponentials modulo a prime, it is very difficult to calculate discrete logarithms.

-

For large primes, calculating discrete logarithms is considered infeasible.

- Because only A and B can determine the key, no other user can read the message (confidentiality).
- Recipient B knows that only user A could have created a message using this key (authentication).
- However, the technique does not protect against replay attacks. One such example is Man-in-the-Middle Attack.

Man-in-the-Middle Attack

- Suppose A and B wish to exchange keys, and E is the attacker.
- The attack proceeds as follows.

- E generates two random private keys X_{E1}andandX_{E2}then computing the corresponding public keys

YE1and **YE2.**

- A transmits **YA** to B.
- E intercepts $Y_A$and transmits ' $Y_{E1}$to B.
- B receives $Y_{E1}$and calculates $K_1 = (Y_{E1})^{XB}$ **mod q.**
- B transmits $Y_B$to A.
- E intercepts $Y_B$and transmits $Y_{E2}$to A.
- A receives$Y_{E2}$and calculates $K_2 = (Y_{E2})^{XA}$ **mod q.**
- E also calculates $K_1 = (Y_B)^{XE1}$**mod** qand $K_2 = (Y_A)^{XE2}$ **mod q**

- At this point, B and A think that they share a secret key, but instead Band E share secret key and A and E share secret key.
- All future communication between B and A is compromised in the following way.

  - A sends an encrypted message **M** as **E(**K_2**, M).**
  - E intercepts the encrypted message and decrypts it to recover M.
  - E sends **E(**K_1**, M)** or **E(**K_1**, M')** to B , where **M'** is any message.

- The key exchange protocol is participants.

vulnerable to such an attack because it does not authenticate the

This vulnerability can be overcome with the use of digital

signatures and public-key certificat

CHAPTER FIVE

Cryptographic Hash Function

Hash Function

- A **hash function** H accepts a variable-length block of data as input and produces a fixed-size hash value.
- A "good" hash function has the property that the results of applying the function to a large set of inputs

will produce outputs that are evenly distributed and apparently random.

- In general terms, the principal object of a hash function is data integrity.
- A change to any bit or bits in results, with high probability, in a change to the hash code.

- Hash function used for security applications is referred to as a **cryptographic hash function.**
- A cryptographic hash function is an algorithm for which it is computationally infeasible to find either
    - A data object that maps to a pre-specified hash result (the one-way property) or
    - Two data objects that map to the same hash result (the collision-free property).
- Because of these characteristics, hash functions are often used to determine whether or not data has changed.
- Figure depicts the general operation of a cryptographic hash function.

Applications of Cryptographic Hash Functions

The range of applications in which it is employed.

Message Authentication

- Message authentication is a mechanism or service used to verify the integrity of a message.
- Message authentication assures that data received are exactly as sent.
- Hash function is used to provide message authentication.
- The hash function value is often referred to as a **message digest**.
- Variety of ways in which a hash code can be used to provide message authentication, as follows.

a. The message plus concatenated hash code is encrypted using symmetric encryption. Because only A and B share the secret key, the message must have come from A and has not been altered. The hash code provides the structure or redundancy required to achieve authentication. Confidentiality is also provided.
b. Only the hash code is encrypted, using symmetric encryption. This reduces the processing burden for those applications that do not require confidentiality.
c. It is possible to use a hash function but no encryption for message authentication. Two communicating parties share a common secret value S. A computes the hash value over the concatenation of M and S and appends the resulting hash value to M. Because B possesses, it can recomputed the hash value to verify. Opponent cannot generate a false message.
d. Confidentiality can be added to the approach of method (c) by encrypting the entire message plus the hash code.

Digital Signatures

- Another important application, which is similar to the message authentication application, is the **digital signature**.
- The operation of the digital signature is similar to that of the MAC.

- In the case of the digital signature, the hash value of a message is encrypted with a user's private key.
- Anyone who knows the user's public key can verify the integrity of the message that is associated with the

digital signature.

- In this case, an attacker who wishes to alter the message would need to know the user's private key.

a. The hash code is encrypted, using public-key encryption with the sender's private key. This provides authentication. It also provides a digital signature, because only the sender could have produced the encrypted hash code.

b. If confidentiality as well as a digital signature is desired, then the message plus the private-key-encrypted hash code can be encrypted using a symmetric secret key.

Other Applications

- Hash functions are commonly used to create a **one-way password file.**
- Hash functions can be used for **intrusion detection** and **virus detection.**
- A cryptographic hash function can be used to construct a **pseudorandom function (PRF)** or a

pseudorandom number generator (PRNG).

Simple Hash Functions

- Two simple, insecure hash functions are shown here.
- All hash functions operate using the following general principles.
    - The input (message, file, etc.) is viewed as a sequence of ***n***-bit blocks.
    - The input is processed one block at a time in an iterative fashion to produce an -bit hash function.

1. First Function

- One of the simplest hash functions is the bit-by-bit exclusive-OR (XOR) of every block.
- This can be expressed as

?? = ??1???2 ⊕ ... ⊕ ???

Where

?? = ?th bit of the hash code, 1 ≤ ? ≤ n

? = number of n – bit blocks in the input

??? = ?th bit in jth block

⊕= XOR operation

- This operation produces a simple parity for each bit position and is known as a longitudinal redundancy check.
- It is reasonably effective for random data as a data integrity check.
- Each n-bit hash value is equally likely.
- Thus, the probability that a data error will result in an unchanged hash value is 2^{-n}.

1. Second Function

- A simple way to improve matters is to perform a one-bit circular shift, or rotation, on the hash value after each block is processed.
- The procedure can be summarized as follows.

    1. Initially set the n-bit hash value to zero.
    2. Process each successive n-bit block of data as follows:

        a. Rotate the current hash value to the left by one bit.
        b. XOR the block into the hash value.

- This has the effect of "randomizing" the input more completely and overcoming any regularities that appear in the input.

- Although the second procedure provides a good measure of data integrity, it is virtually useless for data security.
- When an encrypted hash code is used with a plaintext message, it is an easy matter to produce a new message that yields that hash code.
- Simply prepare the desired alternate message and then append an n-bit block that forces the new message plus block to yield the desired hash code.

Security Requirements for Cryptographic Hash Functions

Requirement

Description

Variable input size

H can be applied to a block of data of any size.

Fixed output size

H produces a fixed-length output.

Efficiency

H(x) is relatively easy to compute for any given x, making both hardware and software

implementations practical.

Preimage resistant (one-way property)

For any given hash value h, it is computationally infeasible to find y such that

H(y) = h.

Second preimage resistant (weak collision resistant)

For any given block x, it is computationally infeasible to find $y \neq x$ with H(y) = H(x).

Collision resistant (strong collision resistant)

It is computationally infeasible to find any pair (x, y) such that $H(x) = H(y)$.

Pseudorandomness

Output of H meets standard tests for pseudorandomness.

Security attack on Cryptographic Hash Function

Brute-Force Attacks

- A brute-force attack does not depend on the specific algorithm but depends only on bit length.

- In the case of a hash function, a brute-force attack depends only on the bit length of the hash value.
- A cryptanalysis in contrast, is an attack based on weaknesses in a particular cryptographic algorithm.
- We look first at brute-force attacks.

Preimage and Second Preimage Attacks

- Adversary wishes to find a value such that H(y) is equal to a given hash value h.
- The brute-force method is to pick values of y at random and try each value until a collision occurs.
- For an m-bit hash value, the level of effort is proportional to 2m.
- Specifically, the adversary would have to try, on average, 2m-1 values of *y* to find one that generates a given hash value h.

Collision Resistant Attacks

- Adversary wishes to find two messages or data blocks, *x* and y, that yield the same hash function: H(x)=H(y).
- This turns out to require considerably less effort than a preimage or second preimage attack.
- The effort required is explained by a mathematical result referred to as the birthday paradox.
- Thus, for an m-bit hash value, if we pick data blocks at random, we can expect to find two data blocks with the same hash value within $\sqrt{2^{?}} = 2^{?/2}$ attempts.
- Yuval proposed the following strategy to exploit the **birthday paradox** in a collision resistant attack

1. The source, A, is prepared to sign a legitimate message x by appending the appropriate m-bit hash code and encrypting that hash code with A's private key.
2. The opponent generates 2m/2 variations x' of x, all of which convey essentially the same meaning, and stores the messages and their hash values.
3. The opponent prepares a fraudulent message y for which A's signature is desired.
4. The opponent generates minor variations y' of y, all of which convey essentially the same meaning. For each y', the opponent computes H(y'), checks for matches with any of the H(x') values, and continues until a match is found.
5. The opponent offers the valid variation to A for signature. This signature can then be attached to the fraudulent variation for transmission to the intended recipient.

Cryptanalysis

- As with encryption algorithms, cryptanalytic attacks on hash functions seek to exploit some property of the algorithm to perform some attack other than an exhaustive search.
- The way to measure the resistance of a hash algorithm to cryptanalysis is to compare its strength to the effort required for a brute-force attack.
- In recent years, there has been considerable effort, and some successes, in developing cryptanalytic attacks on hash functions.
- To understand these, we need to look at the overall structure of a typical secure hash function, indicated in Figure.

- Cryptanalysis of hash functions focuses on the internal structure of f and is based on attempts to find efficient techniques for producing collisions for a single execution of f.
- Once that is done, the attack must take into account the fixed value of IV.
- The attack on f depends on exploiting its internal structure.
- Typically, as with symmetric block ciphers, f consists of a series of rounds of processing, so that the attack involves analysis of the pattern of bit changes from round to round.

Hash Functions Based on Cipher Block Chaining

- A number of proposals have been made for hash functions based on using a cipher block chaining technique, but without using the secret key. One of the first such proposals was that of Rabin.
- Divide a message M into fixed-size blocks M1, M2, ... , MN and use a symmetric encryption system such as DES to compute the hash code G as

?0 = ??????? ?????

?? = ?(??, ??−1)

? = ??

- This is similar to the CBC technique, but in this case, there is no secret key.
- As with any hash code, this scheme is subject to the birthday attack, and if the encryption algorithm is DES and only a 64-bit hash code is produced, then the system is vulnerable.
- Furthermore, another version of the birthday attack can be used even if the opponent has access to only one message and its valid signature and cannot obtain multiple signings.
- Here is the scenario: We assume that the opponent intercepts a message with a signature in the form of an encrypted hash code and that the unencrypted hash code is bits long.

1. Use the algorithm defined at the beginning of this subsection to calculate the unencrypted hash code G.
2. Construct any desired message in the form Q1, Q2, ... , QN-2. 3. Compute ?? = ?(??, ??−1) for 1 ≤ ? ≤ (? − 2).

4. Generate $2^{m/2}$ random blocks; for each block X, compute ?(?, ??−2). Generate an additional $2^{m/2}$

random blocks; for each block Y, compute D (Y, G), where D is the decryption function corresponding to E.

5. Based on the birthday paradox, with high probability there will be an X and Y such that ?(?, ??−2) =

?(?, ?).

6. Form the message Q1, Q2, ... , QN-2, X, Y, This message has the hash code G and therefore can be used with the intercepted encrypted signature.

- This form of attack is known as a **meet-in-the-middle-attack.**
- A number of researchers have proposed refinements intended to strengthen the basic block chaining approach. For example, Davies and Price describe the variation:

?? = ?(??, ??−1)???−1

- Another variation, proposed is

?? = ?(??−1, ??)???

- However, both of these schemes have been shown to be vulnerable to a variety of attacks.

Secure Hash Algorithm (SHA)

- SHA is based on the hash function MD4.
- The algorithm takes as input a message of maximum length of less than 2128bitsand produces a 512-bit message digest.
- The input is processed in 1024-bit blocks.

- The processing consists of the following steps:

1. Append padding bits.

    - The message is padded so that its length is congruent to 896 modulo 1024.
    - The padding consists of a single 1-bit followed by the necessary number of 0-bits.

2. Append length.

    - A block of 128 bits is appended to the message. This block contains the length of the original message (before the padding).
    - The message is now an integer multiple of 1024 bits in length.

- In the figure below, expanded message is represented as the sequence of 1024-bit blocks M1, M2,..., MN and the total length of the expanded message is N x 1024 bits.

3. Initialize hash buffer.

    - A 512-bit buffer is used to hold intermediate and final results of the hash function.

- The buffercan be represented as eight 64-bit registers (a, b, c, d, e, f, g, h).
- These registers are initialized to the 64-bit integers(hexadecimal values) obtained by taking the first sixty-four bits of the fractional parts of the square roots of the first eightprime numbers.

4. Process message in 1024-bit (128-word) blocks.

   - The heart of the algorithm is a module **F**that consists of 80 rounds.

- SHA has 80 rounds.
- Each round takes as input:
  - 512-bit buffer value **(Hi-1)**
  - 64-bit words **W**tobtained from the current data block by message schedule.

  - Additive constant **Kt** which represent the first sixty-four bits of the fractional parts of the cube roots of the first eighty prime numbers.

- The contents of the buffer are updated after every round.

SHA algorithm

- The output of the eightieth round is added modulo 264to the input to the first round (Hi-1) to produce Hi.

5. Output.

- After all *N* 1024-bit blocks have been processed, the output from the Nth stage is the 512-bit message digest.

SHA-512 Round Function

- Each round updates the buffer in the following way:

Where

Message Schedule

- The 64-bit word values Wtare derived from the 1024-bit message.
- The first16 values ofWt are taken directly from the 16 words of the current block. The remaining values are defined as follows:

Message schedule

- The message schedule introduces a great deal of redundancy and interdependence into the message blocksthat are compressed, which complicates the task of finding a different message block that maps to the same compression function output.

CHAPTER SIX

Message Authentication Codes

Message authentication is a mechanism or service used to verify the integrity of a message. Message authentication assures that data received are exactly as sent by (i.e., contain no modification, insertion, deletion, or replay) and that the purported identity of the sender is valid.

Need for Message Authentication

- Following attacks are possible which are the reason why authentication is needed:

1. **Disclosure:** Release of message contents to any person not knowing the secret key.
2. **Traffic analysis:** Discovery of the pattern of traffic between parties. Traffic analysis reveals information like the frequency and length of messages between parties and the communicating parties could be determined.
3. **Masquerade:** Impersonating other person and sending messages.

4. **Content modification:** Changes are made to the contents of a message. Changes may include insertion, deletion, transposition, and modification.
5. **Sequence modification:** Sequence of messages between parties is modified. This attack may include insertion, deletion, and reordering.
6. **Timing modification:** Delay or replay of messages.
7. **Source repudiation:** Denial of transmission of message by source.
8. **Destination repudiation:** Denial of receipt of message by destination.

- Message authentication verifies that received messages come from the alleged source and have not been altered.
- Message authentication may also verify sequencing and timeliness.

Authentication Techniques

- Following techniques are used for authentication:
    - **Hash function:** Hash function maps a message of any length into a fixed-lengthhash value, which serves as the authenticator.
    - **Message encryption:** The ciphertext of the entire message serves as its authenticator.
    - **Message authentication code (MAC):** A MAC is a function of the message and a secretkey that produces a fixed-length value that serves as the authenticator.

- Authentication using message encryption is explained below:

Message Encryption

- **Symmetric Encryption:** A message **M** transmitted from source A to destination B is encrypted using a secret key K shared by A and B.

Confidentiality and authentication with symmetric encryption

- No other party knows the key, and hence **confidentiality** is provided as no other party can recover the plaintext of the message without the knowledge of key.
- The message must have come from A because A is the only other party that possesses *K* and therefore the only other party which can construct cipher text that can be decrypted with *K*. Thus, authentication is provided.

- Furthermore, if *M* is recovered, B knows that none of the bits of *M* have been altered, because an opponent that does not know *K* would not know how to alter bits in the cipher text to produce desired changes in the plaintext. Thus, **data integrity** is also provided.

- If the message contains regular language, then the legitimacy of the message can be determined.
- But if the message contains arbitrary data like binary object file, digitized X-ray, then alteration in the message cannot be determined by simply looking at the messages.
- In that case, plaintext must have some structure like some message based function (one example is checksum) or add TCP header if TCP/IP is being used.
- **Public-Key Encryption:** The source (A) uses the public key **PUb** of the destination (B) to encrypt *M*. Because only B has the corresponding private key **PRb**, only B can decrypt the message. But this scheme provides **confidentiality** but not authentication because any opponent could also use B's public key to encrypt a message, claiming to be A.

Confidentiality using public key encryption

- To provide authentication, A uses its private key to encrypt the message, and B uses A's public key to decrypt it. The message must have come from A because A is the only party that possesses **PRa**. Anyone with **PUa** can decrypt the message. This scheme also provides digital signature because only A could have constructed the cipher text by encrypting it with **PRa**.

Authentication using public key encryption

- If both authentication and confidentiality is needed, then message is encrypted using both **PUa** and **PRa.by**

using its private key to encrypt. Note that this scheme does not provide confidentiality.

Confidentiality and Authentication using public key encryption

- This scheme also requires some structure in plaintext if it contains arbitrary data.

Message Authentication Code /Cryptographic Checksum

- Cryptographic checksum or MAC is a function of the message and a secret key that produces a fixed-length value that serves as the authenticator.

- A MAC function is similar to encryption. One difference is that the MAC algorithm need not be reversible, as in the case of decryption.
- A MAC function is generally a many-to-one function.

Application of MAC

- Three situations in which a message authentication code is used are:

1. Many applications need to broadcast message to a number of destinations.
    - Examples are notification to users that the network is now unavailable or an alarm signal in a military control center.
    - Instead of decrypting message at every node it is cheaper and more reliable to have only one destination responsible for monitoring authenticity.
    - The message is broadcasted in plaintext with an associated message authentication code. The responsible system has the secret key and performs authentication.
    - If a violation occurs, the other destination systems are alerted by a general alarm.
2. One side in the communication has a heavy load and cannot afford the time to decrypt all incoming messages.

- Authentication is carried out on a selective basis. Messages are chosen at random for checking.

3. Authentication of a computer program in plaintext.

    - The computer program can be executed without having to decrypt it every time.
    - However, if a message authentication code were attached to the program, it could be checked whenever assurance is required about the integrity of the program.

Basic Uses of MAC

- A MAC is an authentication technique involves the use of a secret key to generate a small fixed-size block of data, known as a **cryptographic checksum** or MAC. The MAC is then appended to the message.
- Here, sender and receiver share a secret key.
- When A has to send a message to B, it calculates the MAC as a function of the message and the key:

$$MAC = MAC\ (K, M)$$

Where M is plaintext C is the MAC function K is the secret key and

MAC is the message authentication code.

- The message plus MAC are transmitted to the intended recipient.
- The recipient performs the same calculation on the received message, using the same secret key, to generate

a new MAC. The received MAC is compared to the calculated MAC.

Authentication using MAC, no confidentiality

- Since only the receiver and the sender know the secret key, and if the received MAC matches the calculated MAC, then
  - The receiver is assured that the message has not been altered. If an attacker alters the message but does not alter the MAC, then the receiver's calculation of the MAC will differ from the received MAC.
  - The receiver is assured that the message is from the alleged sender. Because no one else knows the secret key.
- Confidentiality can be provided by performing message encryption either after or before the MAC algorithm.
- In both these cases, two separate keys are needed, each of which is shared by the sender and the receiver.

- MAC can be calculated with the message as input and then concatenated to the message. The entire block is then encrypted.

Authentication and confidentiality using MAC

- It is preferable to tie the authentication directly to the plaintext, hence the above method is typically preferred.

- Alternately, the message is encrypted first. Then the MAC is calculated using the resulting cipher text and is concatenated to the cipher text.

Authentication and confidentiality using MAC

Requirements for Message Authentication Codes

- A MAC, also known as a cryptographic checksum, is generated by a function C of the form

? = ???(?, ?)

Where

M is a variable-length message,

K is a secret key shared only by sender and receiver, and

MAC (K, M) is the fixed-length authenticator also called a **tag**.

- The tag is appended to the message at the source at a time when the message is assumed or known to be correct. The receiver authenticates that message by re-computing the tag.
- When an entire message is encrypted for confidentiality, using either symmetric or asymmetric encryption, the security of the scheme generally depends on the bit length of the key.
- Barring some weakness in the algorithm, the opponent must resort to a brute-force attack using all possible keys.
- On average, such an attack will require 2^{k-1} attempts for a k-bit key. In particular, for a cipher text only attack, the opponent, given cipher text C, performs ?? = ?(??, ?) for all possible key values ?? until a ?? is produced that matches the form of acceptable plaintext.
- Then the MAC function should satisfy the following requirements.

1. If an opponent observes M and ???(?, ?), it should be computationally infeasible for the opponent to construct a message M' such that ???(?, ?) = ???(?, ?′).
2. ???(?, ?) should be uniformly distributed in the sense that for randomly chosen messages, M and M', the probability that ???(?, ?) = ???(?, ?′) is 2^{-n}, where n is the number of bits in the tag.
3. Let M' be equal to some known transformation on M. That is, ?′ = ?(?). For example, f may involve inverting one or more specific bits. In that case, Pr[???(?, ?) = ???(?, ?′)] = $2^{-?}$

Security of MACs/ Attacks on MACs

We group attacks on MACs into two categories: brute-force attacks and cryptanalysis.

Brute-Force Attacks

- A brute-force attack on a MAC requires more known message-MAC pairs than a brute-force attack on a hash function.
- There are two types of possible attack:
    - attack the key space
    - attack the MAC value

1. Attacking the key space

- If an attacker can determine the MAC key, then it is possible to generate a valid MAC value for any input.
- Suppose the key size is **k** bits and that the attacker has one known text–tag (MAC) pair.
- The attacker can then compute the **n-bit** tag on the known text for all possible keys.
- At least one key will produce the correct MAC value for the message. Till now, the level of effort is $\mathbf{2^k}$.
- However, the MAC is a many-to-one mapping, so there may be other keys that produce the correct value.
- Thus, if more than one key is found to produce the correct value, additional text–tag pairs must be tested.
- The level of effort becomes less with each additional text–MAC pair and after 2 or 3 levels, a single key is obtained.

2. Attacking the MAC value

    - The attacker will try to generate a valid MAC for a given message or to find a message that matches a given MAC value.
    - Here the level of effort is that of $\mathbf{2^n}$.
    - This attack cannot be conducted off line without further input; the attacker will require chosen text–tag pairs or knowledge of the key.

Cryptanalysis

- Cryptanalytic attacks on MAC algorithms try to exploit some property of the algorithm to perform some attack other than an exhaustive search.

- The way to measure the resistance of a MAC algorithm to cryptanalysis is to compare its strength to the effort required for a brute-force attack.
- An ideal MAC algorithm will require a cryptanalytic effort greater than or equal to the brute-force effort.

MACs Based On Hash Functions: HMAC

- AMAC derived from hash function is called HMAC.
- The reason for developing HMAC were that hash functions incur less overhead than encryption and the code of hash functions is easily and freely available.

•

The overall operation of HMAC is shown below:

1. Append zeros to the left end of *K* to create a **b-bit** string $\mathbf{K}^{+}$.
2. XOR $\mathbf{K}^{+}$with **ipad** to produce the *b*-bit block ***Si***. Value of ipad is 36 in hexadecimal.
3. Append *M* to ***Si***.
4. Apply H to the stream generated in the above step.
5. XOR $\mathbf{K}^{+}$with **opad** to produce the b-bit block ***So***. Value of opad is 5C in hexadecimal.
6. Append the hash result H from step 4 to***So***.
7. Apply H to the stream generated in the above step and output the result.

- XOR with ipad results in flipping one-half of the bits of *K*.
- Similarly, the XOR with opad results in flipping one-half of the bits of*K*, but a different set of bits.

Security of HMAC

- The security of any HMAC function is based on the cryptographic strength of the underlying hash function.
- The security of a MAC function is expressed in terms of the probability of successful forgery with a given amount of time spent by the forger and a given number of message-MAC pairs created with the same key.
- The probability of successful attack on HMAC is equivalent to one of the following attacks on the embedded hash function:
    - The attacker is able to compute an output of the compression function even with an IV that is random, secret, and unknown to the attacker.
    - The attacker finds collisions in the hash function even when the IV is random and secret.

MACS Based on Block Ciphers: Data Authentication Algorithm (DAA)

- The **Data Authentication Algorithm** (DAA), based on DES, has been one of the most widely used MACs for a number of years.

- Security weaknesses in this algorithm have been discovered, and it is being replaced by newer and stronger algorithms.
- The algorithm can be defined as using the cipher block chaining (CBC) mode of operation of DES with an initialization vector of zero.
- The data to be authenticated are grouped into contiguous 64-bit blocks: D1, D2, ..., DN.
- If necessary, the final block is padded on the right with zeroes to form a full 64-bit block.
-

Using the DES encryption algorithm E and a secret key K, a data authentication code (DAC) is calculated as follows:

?1 = ?(?, ?)
?2 = ?(?, [?2??1)
?3 = ?(?, [?3??2)
.

•

•

?? = ?(?, [?????−1)

- The DAC consists of either the entire block ON or the leftmost M bits of the block, with $16 \leq M \leq 64$.

MACS Based on Block Ciphers: Cipher-Based Message Authentication Code (CMAC)

- As was mentioned, DAA has been widely adopted in government and industry.
- MAC is secure under a reasonable set of security criteria, with the following restriction.
    - Only messages of one fixed length of **mn** bits are processed, where **n** is the cipher block size and **m** is a fixed positive integer.
- Black and Rogaway demonstrated that this limitation could be overcome using three keys:
- one key of length **K** to be used at each step of the cipher block chaining and two keys of length **n**, where **k**

  is the key length and **n** is the cipher block length.

- This proposed construction was refined by Iwata and Kurosawa so that the two n-bit keys could be derived from the encryption key.
- This refinement, adopted by NIST, is the **Cipher-based Message Authentication Code** (CMAC) mode of

operation for use with AES and triple DES.

operation of CMAC

- The message is divided into **n** blocks (M1, M2, ..., Mn).
- The algorithm makes use of a k-bit encryption key **K** and an n-bit constant, **K1**.
- For AES, the key size is 128, 192, or 256 bits;
- for triple DES, the key size is 112 or 168 bits.
- CMAC is calculated as follows:

?1 = ?(?, ?1)

?2 = ?(?, [?2??1)

?3 = ?(?, [?3??2)

.

.

.

?? = ?(?, [?????−1??1)

? = ???????(??)

Where

? = message authetication code, also referred to as the tag

???? = bit length of T

???$_?$(?) = the ? leftmost bits of the bit string?

- If the message is not an integer multiple of the cipher block length, then the final block is padded to the right with a 1 and as many 0s as necessary.
- The CMAC operation then proceeds as before, except that a different *n*-bit key *K*2 is used instead of *K*1.
- The two n-bit keys are derived from the k-bit encryption key as follows.

? = ?(?, 0$^?$)

?1 = ? · ?

?2 = ? · ?^{2} = (? · ?) · ?

where multiplication (•) is done in the finite field GF(2^n) and **x** and $\mathbf{x}^2$are first- and second-order polynomials that are elements of GF(2^n).

CHAPTER SEVEN

Digital Signatures

A **digital signature** is an authentication mechanism that enables the creator of a message to attach a code that acts as a signature. Typically the signature is formed by taking the hash of the message and encrypting the message with the creator's private key. The signature guarantees the source and integrity of the message.

Generic Model of the Digital Signature

- Figure above is a generic model of the process of making and using digital signatures.
- Bob can sign a message using a digital signature generation algorithm.
- The inputs to the algorithm are the message and Bob's private key.
- Any other user, say Alice, can verify the signature using a verification algorithm, whose inputs are the

  message, the signature, and Bob's public key.

- In simplified terms, the essence of the digital signature mechanism is shown in Figure below.

Needs of Digital Signature

- Message authentication protects two parties who exchange messages from any third party.
- However, it does not protect the two parties against each other.
- Several forms of dispute between the two are possible.

1. Mary may forge a different message and claim that it came from John. Mary would simply have to create a

message and append an authentication code using the key that John and Mary share.

2. John can deny sending the message. Because it is possible for Mary to forge a message, there is no way to prove that John did in fact send the message.

- Both scenarios are of legitimate concern.
- The sender pretends that the message was never sent.
- In situations where there is not complete trust between sender and receiver, something more than authentication is needed.
- The most attractive solution to this problem is the digital signature.

Properties of Digital Signature

- The digital signature must have the following properties:

1. It must verify the author and the date and time of the signature.
2. It must authenticate the contents at the time of the signature.
3. It must be verifiable by third parties, to resolve disputes.

- Thus, the digital signature function includes the authentication function.

Security of Digital Signature

- Following types of attacks can be possible on digital signature.
- Here A denotes the user whose signature method is being attacked, and C denotes the attacker.

1. **Key-only attack:** C only knows A's public key.
2. **Known message attack:** C is given access to a set of messages and their signatures.
3. **Generic chosen message attack:** C chooses a list of messages before attempting to breaks A's signature scheme, independent of A's public key. C then obtains from A valid signatures for the chosen messages. The attack is generic, because it does not depend on A's public key; the same attack is used against everyone.
4. **Directed chosen message attack:** Similar to the generic attack, except that the list of messages to be signed is chosen after C knows A's public key but before any signatures are seen.
5. **Adaptive chosen message attack:** C is allowed to use A as an "oracle." This means the A may request signatures of messages that depend on previously obtained message–signature pairs.

- If anyone success at breaking a signature scheme can do any of the following with a non-negligible probability:

1. **Total break:** C determines A's private key.
2. **Universal forgery:** C finds an efficient signing algorithm that provides an equivalent way of constructing signatures on arbitrary messages.
3. **Selective forgery:** C forges a signature for a particular message chosen by C.

4. **Existential forgery:** C forges a signature for at least one message. C has no control over the message. Consequently, this forgery may only be a minor nuisance to A.

Digital Signature Requirements

- On the basis of the properties and attacks just discussed, we can formulate the following requirements for a digital signature.

    1. The signature must be a bit pattern that depends on the message being signed.
    2. The signature must use some information unique to the sender to prevent both forgery and denial.
    3. It must be relatively easy to produce the digital signature.
    4. It must be relatively easy to recognize and verify the digital signature.
    5. It must be computationally infeasible to forge a digital signature, either by constructing a new message for an existing digital signature or by constructing a fraudulent digital signature for a given message.
    6. It must be practical to retain a copy of the digital signature in storage.

Direct Digital Signature

- The term **direct digital signature** refers to a digital signature scheme that involves only the communicating parties (source, destination).
- It is assumed that the destination knows the public key of the source.
- Confidentiality can be provided by encrypting the entire message plus signature with a shared secret key (symmetric encryption).
- Note that it is important to perform the signature function first and then an outer confidentiality function.
- In case of dispute, some third party must view the message and its signature.
- If the signature is calculated on an encrypted message, then the third party also needs access to the decryption key to read the original message.
- However, if the signature is the inner operation, then the recipient can store the plaintext message and its signature for later use in dispute resolution.
- The validity of the scheme just described depends on the security of the sender's private key.
- If a sender later wishes to deny sending a particular message, the sender can claim that the private key was lost or stolen and that someone else forged his or her signature.
- Another threat is that some private key might actually be stolen from X at time T.
- The opponent can then send a message signed with X's signature and stamped with a time before or equal to T.
- The universally accepted technique for dealing with these threats is the use of a digital certificate and certificate authorities.

Elgamal Digital Signature Scheme

- The ElGamal signature scheme involves the use of the private key for encryption and the public key for decryption.
- As with ElGamal encryption, the global elements of **ElGamal digital signature** are a prime number **q**

  and **α**, which is a primitive root of **q**.

- User A generates a private/public key pair as follows.

  1. Generate a random integer ??, such that 1 < ?? < ? – 1.
2. Compute ?? = $?^{?}$? ??? ?.
  3. A's private key is ??; A's pubic key is {?, ?, ??}.

- To sign a message **M**, user A first computes the hash ? = ?(?), such that **m** is an integer in the range 0 <

  ? < ? – 1.

- A then forms a digital signature as follows.

1. Choose a random integer K such that 1 < ? < ? – 1 andgcd(?, ? – 1) = 1. That is, K is relatively prime to q-1.
2. Compute ?1 = $?^{?}$??? ?. Note that this is the same as the computation of ?1 for ElGamal encryption.
3. Compute $?^{-1}$??? (? – 1).That is, compute the inverse of K modulo q-1. 4) Compute ?2 = $?^{-1}$(? – ???1)???(? – 1).

   5) The signature consists of the pair (?1, ?2).

- Any user B can verify the signature as follows. 1. Compute ?1 = ?[?]??? ?.

  2. Compute ?2 = (??)[?]1 (?1)[?]2 ??? ?.

- The signature is valid if ?1 = ?2.

Example

- let us start with the q = 19 and α=10
- Alice generates a key pair as follows:

  1. Alice chooses ?? = 16.
  2. Then ?? = ?[?]? ??? ? = 10^{16}??? 19 = 4.
  3. Alice's private key is 16; Alice's pubic key is {?, ?, ??} = {19, 10, 4}.

- Suppose Alice wants to sign a message with hash value ? = 14.

  1) Alice chooses ? = 5, which is relatively prime to ? − 1 = 18. 2) ?1 = ?[?]??? ? = 10^5??? 19 = 3.
  3) $?^{-1}$??? (? − 1) = 5^{-1}??? (19 − 1) = 11.
  4) $?_2$ = $?^{-1}$(? − $?_?$$?_1$)???(? − 1) = 11(14 − (16)(3))???(19 − 1) = −347 ??? 18 = 4.

- Bob can verify the signature as follows.

  1. ?1 = ?[?]??? ? = 10^{14}??? 19 = 16.

2. ?2 = (??)$^{?}$1 (?1)$^{?}$2 ??? ? = $(4)^{3}(3)^{4}$??? 19 = 5184 ??? 19 = 16.

- Thus, the signature is valid.

Schnorr Digital Signature Scheme

- Schnorr signature scheme is based on discrete logarithms.
- The Schnorr scheme minimizes the message-dependent amount of computation required to generate a signature.
- The main work for signature generation does not depend on the message and can be done during the idle time of the processor.
- The message-dependent part of the signature generation requires multiplying a 2n-bit integer with an n- bit integer.
- The scheme is based on using a prime modulus **p**, with **p-1** having a prime Factor **q** of appropriate size.
- The first part of this scheme is the generation of a private/public key pair, which consists of the following steps.

1. Choose primes **p** and **q**, such that **q** is a prime factor of **p-1**.
2. Choose an integer **α**, such that ?$^{?}$ = 1 ??? ?.The values **α**, **p**, and **q** comprise a global public key that can be common to a group of users.
3. Choose a random integer **s** with 0 < ? < ?.This is the user's private key.

4. Calculate $? = ?^{-?}???$?.This is the user's public key.

- A user with private key **s** and public key **v** generates a signature as follows.

1. Choose a random integer **r** with 0 < ? < ? and compute $? = ?^{?}???$?. This computation is a preprocessing stage independent of the message **M** to be signed.
2. Concatenate the message with **x** and hash the result to compute the value **e:** ? = ?(?||?).
3. Compute? = (? + ??)????. The signature consists of the pair **(e, y)**.

- Any other user can verify the signature as follows. 1. Compute $?' = ?^{?}?^{?}???$?.

    2. Verify that ? = ?(?||?').

Digital Signature Standard

- The National Institute of Standards and Technology (NIST) has published Federal Information Processing Standard FIPS 186, known as the Digital Signature Standard (DSS).
- The DSS makes use of the SHA and presents a new digital signature technique, the **Digital Signature Algorithm (DSA).**
- Latest version also incorporates digital signature algorithms based on RSA and on elliptic curve cryptography.

The DSS Approach

- The DSS uses an algorithm that is designed to provide only the digital signature function.
- Unlike RSA, it cannot be used for encryption or key exchange. Nevertheless, it is a public-key technique.

- Figure contrasts the DSS approach for generating digital signatures to that used with RSA.

RSA approach

- In the RSA approach, the message to be signed is input to a hash function that produces a secure hash code of fixed length.
- This hash code is then encrypted using the sender's private key to form the signature.
- Both the message and the signature are then transmitted.
- The recipient takes the message and produces a hash code.
- The recipient also decrypts the signature using the sender's public key.
- If the calculated hash code matches the decrypted signature, the signature is accepted as valid.

DSS approach

- The DSS approach also makes use of a hash function.
- The hash code is provided as input to a signature function along with a random number k, generated for this particular signature.
- The signature function also depends on the sender's private key (PRa), and a set of parameters known to a group of communicating principals.
- We can consider this set to constitute a global public key (PUG).
- The result is a signature consisting of two components, labeled *s* and *r*.

- At the receiving end, the hash code of the incoming message is generated.
- This plus the signature is input to a verification function.
- The verification function also depends on the global public key as well as the sender's public key (PUa), which is paired with the sender's private key.
- The output of the verification function is a value that is equal to the signature component r, if the signature is valid.
- The signature function is such that only the sender, with knowledge of the private key, could have produced the valid signature.

The Digital Signature Algorithm

-

The DSA is based on the difficulty of computing discrete logarithms and is based on schemes originally presented by ElGamal and Schnorr.

- Figure summarizes the algorithm.

Global Public-Key Components

- There are three parameters that are public and can be common to a group of users.
- A 160-bit prime number **q** is chosen.
- Next, a prime number **p** is selected with a length between 512 and 1024 bits such that **q** divides **(*p* - 1)**.
- Finally, *g* is chosen to be of the form $h^{(?-1)/?}$??? ?, where *h* is an integer between 1 and **(*p* - 1)** with the restriction that **g** must be greater than 1.

User's Private Key

- With these numbers in hand, each user selects a private key and generates a public key.
- The private key **x** must be a number from 1 to **(*q* - 1)** and should be chosen randomly.

User's Public Key

- The public key is calculated from the private key as shown in figure.
- It should be computationally infeasible to determine **x**, from **y**.

User's Per-Message Secrete Number

- Random number k is integer with 0 < k <q.

Creating Signature

- To create a signature, a user calculates two quantities, **r** and **s**, that are functions of the public key components **(p, q, g)**, the user's private key **x**, the hash code of the message H(M), and an additional integer **k** that should be generated randomly and be unique for each signing.

Verification

- At the receiving end, verification is performed using the formulas shown in Figure.
- The receiver generates a quantity that is a function of the public key components, the sender's public key,

  and the hash code of the incoming message.

- If this quantity matches the component of the signature, then the signature is validated.
- Figure below depicts the functions of signing and verifying.

9 798886 672800

Printed by Libri Plureos GmbH in Hamburg,
Germany